Mumbai's Roadside Snacks

Tarla Dalal
■ INDIA'S #1 COOKERY AUTHOR ■

S&C

SANJAY & CO.

MUMBAI

COOK BOOKS BY TARLA DALAL

INDIAN COOKING

Tava Cooking
Rotis & Subzis
Desi Khana
The Complete Gujarati Cook Book
Mithai
Chaat
Achaar aur Parathe
The Rajasthani Cookbook
Swadisht Subzian
Punjabi Khana [New]
Mughlai Khana [New]
South Indian Recipes [New]

TOTAL HEALTH

Low Calorie Healthy Cooking
Pregnancy Cookbook
Baby and Toddler Cookbook
Cooking with 1 Teaspoon of Oil
Home Remedies
Delicious Diabetic Recipes
Fast Foods Made Healthy
Healthy Soups & Salads
Healthy Breakfast
Calcium Rich Recipes
Healthy Heart Cook Book
Forever Young Diet
Healthy Snacks
Iron Rich Recipes
Healthy Juices
Low Cholesterol Recipes
Good Food for Diabetes

Healthy Subzis
Healthy Snacks for Kids
High Blood Pressure Cook Book
Low Calorie Sweets
Nutritious Recipes for Pregnancy
Diabetic Snacks
Zero Oil Rotis & Subzis
Zero Oil Soups, Salads & Snacks
Zero Oil Dal & Chawal
Acidity Cook Book
Growing Kids Cookbook
Soya Rotis & Subzis
Cooking with Sprouts
Exotic Diabetic Cooking - Part 1 [New]
Healthy Diabetic Cooking [New]
Protein Rich Recipes [New]
Eat Well Stay Well [New]

WESTERN COOKING

The Complete Italian Cookbook
The Chocolate Cookbook
Eggless Desserts
Mocktails & Snacks
Thai Cooking
Soups & Salads
Mexican Cooking
Chinese Cooking
Easy Chinese Cooking
Sizzlers & Barbeques
Cakes & Pastries [New]
Party Drinks [New]
Wraps & Rolls [New]

MINI SERIES

Cooking Under 10 minutes
Pizzas and Pasta
Fun Food for Children
Roz ka Khana
Idlis & Dosas
Microwave - Desi Khana
Paneer
Parathas
Chawal
Dals
Sandwiches
Quick Cooking
Curries & Kadhis
Chinese Recipes
Jain Desi Khana
7 Dinner Menus
Jain International Recipes
Punjabi Subzis

Chips & dips
Corn
Microwave Subzis
Baked Dishes
Stir-Fry
Potatoes
Recipes Using Leftovers
Noodles
Lebenese
Cook Book for Two's
Know your Dals & Pulses
Fruit & Vegetable Carving
Know your Spices
Know your Flours
Popular Restaurant Gravies
Paneer Snacks [New]
Know Your Green Leafy Vegetables [New]
Pressure Cooker Recipes [New]

GENERAL COOKING

Exciting Vegetarian Cooking
Microwave Recipes
Saatvik Khana
The Pleasures of Vegetarian Cooking
The Delights of Vegetarian Cooking
The Joys of Vegetarian Cooking
Cooking with Kids
Snacks Under 10 Minutes
Ice-Cream & Frozen Desserts
Desserts Under 10 Minutes
Entertaining
Microwave Snacks & Desserts
Kebabs & Tikkis [New]
Non-fried Snacks [New]

Second Printing : 2010

Copyright © Sanjay & Co.

ISBN : 978-81-89491-66-6

Price Rs. 299/-

Published & Distributed by :
SANJAY & COMPANY
353/A-1, Shah & Nahar Industrial Estate, Dhanraj Mill Compound, Lower Parel (W), Mumbai - 400 013. INDIA.
Tel. : (91-22) 4345 2400 • Fax : (91-22) 2496 5876 • E-mail : sanjay@tarladalal.com • E-mail : www.tarladalal.com

For book purchase enquiry & tarladalal.com membership, call our Toll Free Number : 1 800 209 3252
from any landline or mobile in India.

UK and USA customers can call us on :
UK : 02080029533 • USA : 213-634-1406
For books, Membership on **tarladalal.com**, Subscription for **Cooking & More** and Recipe queries
Timing : 9.30 a.m. to 7.00 p.m. (IST), from Monday to Saturday
Local call charges applicable

Recipe Research, & Production Design
Nisha Katira
Sapna Kamdar
Preetha Srinivasan

Design
Satyamangal Rege

Photography
Payal Choksi

Food Stylist
Arati Fedane

Copy Editor
Janani Gopalkrishnan Vikram

Typesetting
Adityas Enterprises

Printed by
Minal Sales Agencies, Mumbai

Introduction

I'm quite passionate about eating out... and this means everything from five-star restaurants and coffee shops to the new-age boutique restaurants. However, to this day, the most satisfying indulgence remains the street food of India! Those who have not tasted this, fussing about hygiene and nutritive value, have really missed something good in life. Street food is extremely popular in India, mainly because you can have a wholesome meal at half the price of any comparable dish in a restaurant. Be it a nutritious quick lunch, take-away food, snacks, fast food or even junk food, these can be purchased on any foot path, beach-side or road corner. However, wherever you are, you will surely find a large selection of scrumptious snacks, each prepared more temptingly than the other. While street food is popular all over India, Mumbai, more than any other Indian city, finds expression in its streets. Mumbai has people belonging to various economic classes. Thousands of working families survive on a diet of street food! And this is no compromise, because most often the vendors on the street match or surpass the taste of food offered by high-class eateries!

In fact, some of the vendors gain such a reputation for their snacks that people will journey far to experience the food from a specific vendor. Orders come pouring in as the vendor prepares freshly-fried or mixed snacks right in front of your eyes. He never seems overwhelmed however high the order-load is! What is more, he also caters to everybody's preferences.... *"Bhaiyyaaa...zara theeka kam banana"*, *"Aur ek papdi do na"*, *"Ek Jain sandwich banana"*... everybody is heard and served with equal attention! Whether it is a good old lazy Sunday, a festive season or simply a normal working day, the street side is always packed with hungry people waiting for more. Smartly-dressed guys in ties and formals will be relishing *pani puri*, right next to a *rikshah-wala* enjoying the dish with equal gusto! Rich and poor of all ages forget their differences and enjoy the feast, not bothering overly about sophistication, ambience and other niceties. Not surprisingly, Mumbai's street food entices not just the locals but the tourists too. Another interesting aspect is how the street food *wallahs* are always busy! There are some nocturnal vendors who do their business from 10 p.m. to 5 a.m. just selling bun *maska*, jam butter *maska* (buttered buns) and hot tea/coffee. This is a treat for the average Mumbaikar who toils at night when the rest of us are already in bed. So, there is always some food option for everyone in Mumbai. Nobody goes hungry.

Like most things, street food in Mumbai has also undergone changes. For ages, it was ruled by the *wada pav* and *dosas*, along with the standard cutting *chai*, *bhel* and bun *maska*. But with time and changing tastes, not only do we now see a wide range of new foods, but also revamped versions of the all-time favourites. *Dosa* gave birth to Chopsuey *dosa*, and bhel accommodated variations such as Chinese *bhel* and corn *bhel*! New wonders like Frankies, *khichai papad* and grilled sandwiches found a place on the streets of Mumbai. Just like the city that expands to accommodate anybody who comes to it with hope, the city's street food scene has also adapted, imbibing the best of several cuisines from Western to Oriental! Not just the food, but even the serving options and packaging styles are being constantly upgraded. Vendors now offer tissues in lieu of newspaper pieces, which were earlier used. You can get your grilled sandwich packed crisply in a nice aluminium foil rather than in the bread packet paper used to pack sandwiches in the past. Whatever be the packing style, the Mumbaikar makes the most of any good food available at an affordable rate! It is not surprising that anything innovatively presented or made in a jiffy at a moderate price and proportion works well in Mumbai. Some foods like *golas*, *pani puri* etc. are best had at the roadside, for the sheer fun! The kind of happiness and joy one has eating these finger-licking delicacies at the stall cannot be compared to eating at home. However, for those who wish to reproduce the magic of the street-side vendor in their own kitchen, this book serves as a guiding light, presenting the basic technique of making each dish, apart from capturing the intricacies of each street food and taking you for a walk along the Mumbai roads, showing you the foodie's favourite spots and even the price range of each food! Walk alongside me as we explore the streets of Mumbai! Recreate the magic on your kitchen table… but don't forget to put aside your expensive China crockery and bring out the paper plates, to bring alive the true spirit of street food! Dig in!

Best wishes,

Index

Idlis & Dosas...32

Sandwiches...50

Travel all around India, but you cannot find a more lovable dish than Mumbai's wada pav! Truly the "poor man's burger", it is satiating, tasty and affordable, and finds a place even in high-end food courts. In fact, many rely on a standard meal of Wada pav or kaanda bhajji... perhaps because they are short of time or cash – or simply because they cannot resist the temptation!

A yummy mashed potato patty, spiced with green chillies, ginger and other spices, is dipped in a batter of besan and spices and deep-fried. Finally, it is sandwiched between pav and drizzled with teekha and meetha chutneys. The spiced lehsun chutney is the key add-on! The cart vendor has more to offer... frills such as samosas and bhajjis along with deep-fried chillies that add zest to the already tempting feast.

Dabeli is one such variation of this all-time favourite, which ends up as a truly wholesome meal, thanks to the add-ons such as spiced dabeli masala, peanuts etc. The thali is garnished enticingly with chopped grapes, pomegranates, and grated and coloured khopra. Devour this delight raw or grilled in butter!

How easy on the pocket: Rs. 6 to Rs. 10

A few areas you just can't afford to miss:

CTO at Fountain, Churchgate • Kirti College • Anna at Mithibai College • Kunj Vihar Wada Pav, Thane - West • Mulund Kutchi Dabeli • Krishna Wada, Dadar • Kandivali Chowpatty, S. V. Road.

Pav Snacks

WADA PAV

Aptly called the poor man's burger! Deep-fried potato patties served between laddi pav smeared with an assortment of chutneys, this serves as a meal at a meagre price of just Rs 5 to Rs 10. Serve with fried green chillies if you like stuff a tad spicier, and perk it up further by adding finely chopped onions along with the chutneys.

Preparation Time: 35 minutes. **Cooking Time:** 20 minutes. **Makes** 4 *wada pav.*

For the *wada*
2 green chillies, finely chopped
½ tsp finely chopped ginger *(adrak)*
1 tsp finely chopped garlic *(lehsun)*
1 tsp oil
½ tsp mustard seeds *(rai/ sarson)*
¼ tsp asafoetida *(hing)*
5 to 7 curry leaves *(kadi patta)*
1½ cups boiled, peeled and mashed potatoes
A pinch turmeric powder *(haldi)*
Salt to taste
Oil for deep-frying

To be mixed together into a smooth batter
⅓ cup *besan* (Bengal gram flour)
A pinch turmeric powder *(haldi)*
Salt to taste
¼ cup water

For the *meetha chutney* (makes approx. 3½ cups)
1 cup deseeded dates *(khajur)*
2 to 3 tbsp deseeded tamarind *(imli)*
½ cup grated jaggery *(gur)*
½ tsp chilli powder
1 tsp cumin seeds *(jeera)* powder
Salt to taste

For the *teekha chutney* (makes approx. 1 cup)
1 cup roughly chopped coriander *(dhania)*
4 to 5 green chillies, roughly chopped
2 tsp chopped ginger *(adrak)*
1 tsp lemon juice
Salt to taste

For the *sukha lehsun ka chutney* (makes approx. ½ cup)

⅓ cup peeled garlic cloves *(lehsun)*
¼ cup grated dried coconut *(kopra)*
2 tbsp chilli powder
1 tsp coriander seeds *(dhania)* powder
1 tsp oil
Salt to taste

For serving

4 *laddi pav*
Meetha chutney, page 10
Teekha chutney, page 10
Sukha lehsun ka chutney, refer above
8 to 10 fried green chillies, refer handy tip

For the *wada*

1. Combine the green chillies, ginger and garlic and pound using a mortar-pestle *(khalbhatta)*. Keep aside.
2. Heat the oil in a small *kadhai* and add the mustard seeds.
3. When the seeds crackle, add the asafoetida and curry leaves and sauté on a medium flame for a few seconds.
4. Add the pounded mixture and sauté on a medium flame for a few more seconds.
5. Add the potatoes, turmeric powder and salt, mix well and cook for a minute, while stirring continuously. Remove from the flame and keep aside to cool.
6. Divide the mixture into 4 equal portions and shape each portion into a flat round.
7. Dip each *wada* in the prepared batter and deep-fry in hot oil till they turn golden brown in colour from all the sides. Drain on absorbent paper and keep aside.

For the *meetha chutney*

1. Combine the dates, tamarind, jaggery and 1 cup of water, mix well and pressure cook for 2 to 3 whistles.
2. Allow the steam to escape before opening the lid. Keep aside to cool.

3. Blend in a mixer to a smooth paste and strain using a strainer.
4. Add 1½ cups of water, chilli powder, cumin seeds powder and salt and mix well.
5. Use as required and store the remaining in an air-tight container in a deep-freezer.

For the *teekha chutney*

1. Combine all the ingredients, add ¼ cup of water and blend in a mixer till smooth.
2. Use as required and store the remaining in an air-tight container in a deep-freezer.

For the *sukha lehsun ka chutney*

1. Pound the garlic in a mortar-pestle *(khalbhatta)* till smooth.
2. Transfer it to a bowl, add the dried coconut, chilli powder, coriander seeds powder, oil and salt and mix well.
3. Use as required and store the remaining in an air-tight container in the refrigerator.

How to serve

1. Slit a *pav* horizontally, apply *meetha chutney*, *teekha chutney* and *sukha lehsun ka chutney* (as per your taste) on the inner sides of the *pav* and stuff with a hot *wada*.
2. Repeat with the remaining ingredients to make 3 more *wada pav*.
   Serve immediately with fried green chillies.

Handy tip:

Deep-fry the green chillies in hot oil till they turn slightly whitish in colour and crisp. Drain on absorbent paper and serve.

SAMOSA PAV

An equally popular brother of the famous wada pav! Deep-fried samosas with a spicy potato and peas filling are sandwiched between laddi pav flavoured with chutneys. It has now become savvy to grill the samosa pav a little and serve it hot. The crisp outer crust of the samosa entices the diner to have one more, and perhaps even one more!

Preparation Time: 25 minutes. **Cooking Time:** 15 minutes. **Makes** 4 *samosa pav.*

For the dough
1/3 cup plain flour *(maida)*
1/2 tsp melted ghee
A pinch carom seeds *(ajwain)*
Salt to taste

For the stuffing
1 tbsp oil
1/2 tsp cumin seeds *(jeera)*
A pinch asafoetida *(hing)*
2 tsp ginger-green chilli paste
5 to 6 medium sized potatoes, boiled, peeled and cut into cubes
2 tbsp *hara vatana* (dried green peas), soaked and boiled / boiled fresh green peas
1/4 tsp whole coriander seeds *(dhania)*
1/4 tsp dry mango powder *(amchur)*
1 tsp *garam masala*
1 tbsp chopped coriander *(dhania)*
Salt to taste

Other ingredients
Oil for deep-frying

For serving
4 *laddi pav*
Meetha chutney, page 10
Teekha chutney, page 10
Sukha lehsun ka chutney, page 11
8 to 10 fried green chillies, page 11

For the dough
1. Combine all the ingredients in a bowl and knead into a semi-stiff dough using enough water. Cover the dough with a wet muslin cloth and keep aside for 5 minutes.
2. Knead again till smooth and elastic and divide the dough into 2 equal portions. Cover with a wet muslin cloth and keep aside.

For the stuffing
1. Heat the oil in a deep pan or *kadhai* and add the cumin seeds.
2. When the seeds crackle, add the asafoetida and ginger-green chilli paste and sauté on a medium flame for a few seconds.
3. Add the potatoes, *vatana* / green peas, coriander seeds, dry mango powder, *garam masala*, coriander and salt, mix well and cook on a medium flame for a minute, while stirring continuously.
4. Remove from the flame, mash lightly using the back of a spoon and divide the stuffing into 4 equal portions. Keep aside.

How to proceed
1. Roll out a portion of the dough into 150 mm. x 75 mm. (6" x 3") diameter oval.
2. Cut the oval horizontally into 2 equal portions using a knife (refer the diagram on page 13).

3. Take a portion and join the edges to make a cone, stuff each cone with a portion of the stuffing and apply little water on the edges and fold to seal it (as shown in the diagram given below).
4. Repeat with the remaining dough and stuffing to make 3 more *samosas*.
5. Heat the oil in a *kadhai*, and deep-fry the *samosas* on a medium flame till they turn golden brown in colour. Drain on absorbent paper. Keep aside.

How to serve

1. Slit a *pav* horizontally, apply *meetha chutney*, *teekha chutney* and *sukha lehsun ka chutney* (as per your taste) on the inner sides of the *pav* and stuff with a hot *samosa*.
2. Repeat with the remaining ingredients to make 3 more *samosa pav*.
   Serve immediately with fried green chillies.

BHAJJI PAV

The westerner would never have imagined such an Indian version of the sandwich! Thinly-sliced potatoes are dipped in a besan batter and deep-fried. A stack of six to seven such crisp bhajjis are sandwiched in pav, to make a veritable feast! A good option for those who love street food but prefer to stay away from spices.

Preparation Time: 10 minutes.　**Cooking Time:** 20 minutes.　**Makes** 4 *bhajji pav.*

For the *bhajji*
½ cup *besan* (Bengal gram flour)
¼ tsp turmeric powder *(haldi)*
Salt to taste
3 medium sized potatoes, peeled and thinly sliced
Oil for deep-frying

For serving
4 *laddi pav*
Meetha chutney, page 10
Teekha chutney, page 10
Sukha lehsun ka chutney, page 11
8 to 10 fried green chillies, page 11

For the *bhajji*
1. Combine the *besan*, turmeric powder, salt and ¼ cup of water in a bowl and mix well to make a smooth batter of pouring consistency.

2. Heat the oil in a *kadhai*, dip a few potato slices in the batter and deep-fry till they turn light brown in colour and crisp from all the sides. Drain on absorbent paper.
3. Repeat with the remaining potato slices and batter to make more *bhajjis*.

How to serve
1. Slit a *pav* horizontally, apply *meetha chutney*, *teekha chutney* and *sukha lehsun ka chutney* (as per your taste) on the inner sides of the *pav* and stuff it with 6 to 7 hot *bhajjis*.
2. Repeat with the remaining ingredients to make 3 more *bhajji pav*.
   Serve immediately with fried green chillies.

VARIATION:
PALAK BHAJJI PAV

To make one plate of *palak bhajji pav*, dip 6 to 7 de-stemmed baby spinach leaves in the *besan* batter and deep-fry till they turn brown and crisp on all the sides. Proceed as per the above recipe.

KAANDA BHAJJI PAV

The Mumbaiite is no stranger to 'kanda bhajia'. You must try it too! Thinly-sliced onions are flavoured with spices and deep-fried in hot oil. You can serve six to eight bhajjis per plate, either as is, or sandwiched between a sliced pav! Must be had piping hot!

Preparation Time: 10 minutes.   **Cooking Time:** 20 minutes.   **Makes** 4 *bhajji pav*.

For the *kaanda bhajji*

2 cups thinly sliced onions
1¼ cups *besan* (Bengal gram flour)
1½ tbsp whole coriander seeds *(dhania)*, coarsely ground
1 to 2 green chillies, finely chopped
1 tsp chilli powder
½ tsp turmeric powder *(haldi)*
2 tbsp finely chopped coriander *(dhania)*
Salt to taste
Oil for deep-frying

For serving

4 *laddi pav*
Sukha lehsun ka chutney, page 11
8 to 10 fried green chillies, page 11

For the *kaanda bhajji*

1. Combine all the ingredients in a bowl, add ¼ cup of water and mix well.

2. Heat the oil in a *kadhai* and drop ¼th of the mixture, while spreading it evenly using your fingers to form small lumps.
3. Deep-fry till they turn golden brown in colour and crisp from all sides.
4. Repeat with the remaining mixture to make 3 more batches of *bhajjis*. Drain on absorbent paper.

How to serve

1. Place equal portions of hot *bhajjis* on 4 individual plates and serve immediately with *laddi pav*, *sukha lehsun ka chutney* and fried green chillies.
2. Alternatively stuff the *bhajjis* in *pav* as shown in the image.

15

VATI DAL NA BHAJIYA

When you don't want to have something as heavy as a pav snack, switch to these petite moong dal bhajjis. The crushed peppercorns and coriander seeds give these crisp dumplings their characteristic flavour.

Preparation Time: 10 minutes.   **Cooking Time:** 15 minutes.   **Makes** 4 plates.
Soaking Time: 1½ to 2 hours.

For the *bhajiya*
1 cup yellow *moong dal* (split yellow gram)
2 green chillies, roughly chopped
7 to 8 black peppercorns *(kali mirch),* coarsely crushed
1 tsp whole coriander seeds *(dhania),* coarsely crushed
Salt to taste
Oil for deep-frying

For serving
Meetha chutney, page 10
Teekha chutney, page 10
Sukha lehsun ka chutney, page 11

For the *bhajiya*
1. Clean, wash and soak the *moong dal* in enough water for atleast 1½ to 2 hours.

2. Drain, add the green chillies and grind in a mixer to a coarse paste using enough water.
3. Transfer the mixture to a bowl, add the peppercorns, coriander seeds and salt and mix well.
4. Heat the oil in a *kadhai*, drop spoonful of mixture in it and deep-fry till they turn light brown in colour and crisp from all sides.
5. Repeat with the remaining mixture to make more *bhajiyas*. Drain on absorbent paper.

How to serve
Place equal portions of hot *bhajiyas* on 4 plates and serve immediately with *meetha chutney, teekha chutney* and *sukha lehsun ka chutney.*

BREAD PAKODA

Love it or hate it, but you definitely can't ignore it, as this quick snack is all over Mumbai! Aloo bhaji/masala is sandwiched between two slices of bread and deep-fried in a flavoured besan batter. At Rs. 10 per plate, what more can you ask for?

Preparation Time: 10 minutes. **Cooking Time:** 20 minutes. **Makes** 4 plates.

To be mixed into a smooth batter
1 cup *besan* (Bengal gram flour)
½ cup water
¼ tsp turmeric powder *(haldi)*
½ tsp chilli powder
2 pinches asafoetida *(hing)*
Salt to taste

Other ingredients
4 big slices bread
1 recipe *aloo masala*, page 54 (refer handy tip)
Oil for deep-frying

For serving
Meetha chutney, page 10
Teekha chutney, page 10
Sukha lehsun ka chutney, page 11
8 to 10 fried green chillies, page 11

1. Place a slice of bread on a clean flat surface and spread ½ of the *aloo masala* evenly over it.
2. Place another slice of bread over it, press lightly and cut it diagonally into 2 equal pieces.
3. Repeat with the remaining ingredients to make 2 more pieces.

4. Dip each piece in the batter till it is evenly coated from all the sides, slide in hot oil and deep-fry on a medium flame till they turn light brown in colour and crisp from all sides. Drain on absorbent paper.

How to serve
1. Place a piece on a plate and serve immediately with *meetha chutney, teekha chutney, sukha lehsun ka chutney* and fried green chillies.
2. Repeat with the remaining ingredients to make 3 more plates.

Handy tip:
You may avoid using green peas in *aloo masala* for this recipe.

VARIATION:
Make these *pakodas* without the stuffing! Apply *teekha chutney* and *sukha lehsun ka chutney* between the bread slices, coat with batter and deep-fry.

DABELI

A spicy potato mixture combined with onions, garlic chutney, meetha chutney, spiced masala peanuts and fruits like pomegranates and grapes... how can the equation go wrong! Serve plain or smeared with butter and grilled on a tava! Since dabeli masala is available in provision stores, you can easily recreate the roadside experience.

Preparation Time: 10 minutes.   **Cooking Time:** 20 minutes.   **Makes** 4 *dabeli*.

For the stuffing
1½ tbsp *dabeli masala* (readily available in the market)
2 tbsp *meetha chutney*, page 10
2 tsp oil
½ cup boiled, peeled and mashed potatoes
Salt to taste
1 tbsp desiccated coconut
1 tbsp finely chopped coriander *(dhania)*
2 tbsp fresh pomegranate *(anar)*
2 tbsp chopped green grapes

For the *geela lehsun ka chutney* (makes approx. ¾ cup)
1 cup peeled and roughly chopped garlic *(lehsun)*
3 tbsp chilli powder
Salt to taste

Other ingredients
4 *dabeli pav*
2 tsp *geela lehsun ka chutney*, recipe above
2 tbsp *meetha chutney*, page 10
4 tsp finely chopped onions
4 tsp *masala* peanuts (readily available in the market)
4 tsp Nylon *sev,* refer handy tip, page 19
2 tsp butter for cooking

For the stuffing
1. Combine the *dabeli masala* and *meetha chutney* in a bowl and mix well.
2. Heat the oil in a pan or *kadhai,* add the *dabeli masala* and *chutney* mixture, mix well and sauté for a few seconds.

3. Add the potatoes, salt and 2 tbsp of water, mix well and cook on a medium flame for 2 minutes, while stirring continuously.
4. Transfer to a *thali,* sprinkle coconut, coriander, pomegranate and grapes evenly over it. Keep aside.

For the *geela lehsun ka chutney*
1. Combine all the ingredients, add ¼ cup of water and blend in a mixer to a smooth paste.
2. Use as required and store the remaining in an air-tight container in the refrigerator.

How to proceed
1. Take a *pav* and slit it on two sides at right angle (keeping them joined at the remaining 2 ends).
2. Apply ½ tsp of *geela lehsun ka chutney* and 1½ tsp of *meetha chutney* evenly on the inner sides of the *pav.*
3. Stuff with 1½ tbsp of the stuffing and top it with 1 tsp of onions, 1 tsp of *masala* peanuts and 1 tsp of *sev.*
4. Repeat with the remaining ingredients to make 3 more *dabeli.*
5. Just before serving, cook each *dabeli* on a hot *tava* (griddle) for a minute using ½ tsp of butter. Serve immediately.

VARIATION:
JAIN DABELI

To make a Jain version of this snack, simply replace potatoes with an equal quantity of raw bananas to make the stuffing. While serving, do not apply *geela lehsun ka chutney* to the *pav*. For the rest, proceed as per the recipe.

Handy tip:

Nylon *sev* is a variety of deep-fried *besan* (Bengal gram) *sev,* which is very thin and crisp. It adds crunch to the recipe and is thus used as a topping for *chaats*. It is readily available at most provision stores.

Chatpata Chaat

Chaat has become almost synonymous with street food! It defines the food culture of Mumbai, bhel puri and pani puri being the city's signature dishes!

Hmm, let us start with a bhel. Kurmure served with a spicy mixture of chopped veggies and spices, topped with khajur imli chutney, teekha lehsun chutney, a dash of lime juice, sprinkled with rock salt, etc. Drooling already? Wait till you taste the pani puri!

Crisp out of bubbling oil, the pani puri's frail crust gives way as soon as you eat it, flooding your mouth with cool, mint-spiked water, lovingly called phudine ka pani and khajur imli ki chutney. The trick is to devour the pani puri as quickly as the bhaiyyah (as the vendor is lovingly called in Mumbai) deftly constructs them, and before the rich juices trickle down your wrist.

Once your appetite is all charged up, you can dig into whatever else the vendor has on to offer, be it the sumptuous, hot ragda patties or other delightful combinations such as the dahi puri or ragda puri.

How easy on the pocket: Rs. 10 to Rs. 15

A few areas you just can't afford to miss:

Hari Om Bhelwala, Fort • Vithal, VT • Parle Station, West • Juhu beach • Chowpatty • Matunga Panipuriwala, East • Kandivali Chowpatty, S. V. Road.

GEELA BHEL

Kurmura (puffed rice) is combined deftly with a mélange of spices, veggies and chutneys in a paper cone and then topped with a fresh squeeze of lemon juice, masala, coriander, sev and papadi. The papadi acts as an edible spoon, which can be gobbled up as a crunchy finale!

Preparation Time: 10 minutes.　**Cooking Time:** Nil.　**Makes** 4 plates.

For the *teekha phudina chutney* (makes approx. 1½ cups)
2 cups chopped coriander (dhania)
1 cup chopped mint leaves (phudina)
7 to 8 green chillies, roughly chopped
½ tsp cumin seeds (jeera)
½ tsp fennel seeds (saunf)
3 to 4 black peppercorns (kalimirch)
1 clove (laung/lavang)
25 mm. (1") piece ginger (adrak)
1 tbsp lemon juice
1 tsp black salt (sanchal)
Salt to taste

For the dry *masala* powder (makes approx. ⅓ cup)
½ cup cumin seeds (jeera), roasted
2 tbsp black peppercorns (kalimirch)
¼ tsp cloves (laung/lavang)
¼ cup salt
2 tbsp black salt (sanchal)

Other ingredients
4 cups puffed rice (kurmura)
½ cup chopped onions
½ cup boiled, peeled and chopped potatoes
½ cup Nylon sev, page 19
6 to 8 papadis/puris, crushed
4 tsp masala dal, refer handy tip, page 23
1 tbsp finely chopped raw mangoes (optional)
8 to 10 tbsp meetha chutney, page 10
3 to 4 tbsp teekha phudina chutney, recipe above

4 tsp geela lehsun ka chutney, page 18
¾ tsp dry masala powder, recipe besides
1 tbsp lemon juice

For the garnish
½ cup Nylon sev, page 19
4 tsp masala dal, refer handy tip, page 23
4 tsp chopped coriander (dhania)

For serving
4 papadis

For the *teekha phudina chutney*
Combine all the ingredients, add ½ cup of water and blend in a mixer to a smooth paste. Use as required and store the remaining in an air-tight container in deep-freezer.

For the dry *masala* powder
1. Combine the cumin seeds, peppercorns and cloves and blend in a mixer to a fine powder.
2. Transfer to a bowl, add the salt and black salt and mix well. Use as required and store the remaining in an air-tight bottle.

How to proceed
1. Combine all the ingredients in a large bowl and mix well.
2. Place equal portions of *bhel* on 4 plates and garnish each plate with 2 tbsp of *sev*, 1 tsp of *masala dal* and 1 tsp of coriander.
   Serve immediately with *papadis*.

Handy tip:

Masala dal is readily available at most provision stores or can be made at home. Soak the *chana dal* for at least 4 to 5 hours, drain, deep-fry in hot oil and toss in a mixture of salt, chilli powder and black salt. It is added to increase flavour and add crunch to *chaats*.

SUKHA BHEL

The best medicine for sudden hunger pangs, be it on a noisy railway platform or a quiet roadside! This dry, non-messy variation of bhel can be stuffed in as a quick meal even as you rush to work. You may add veggies like tomatoes etc if you wish to make it an even more enjoyable and wholesome snack.

Preparation Time: 15 minutes.　　**Cooking Time:** Nil.　　**Makes** 4 plates.

To be coarsely ground into *sukha teekha chutney*
1½ tbsp *daria dal* (split roasted Bengal gram)
1 tbsp puffed rice (*kurmura*)
2 to 3 green chillies, roughly chopped
1 cup chopped mint leaves (*phudina*)
¼ cup chopped coriander (*dhania*)
1 tsp lemon juice
A pinch turmeric powder (*haldi*)
A pinch asafoetida (*hing*)
Salt to taste

Other ingredients
4 cups puffed rice (*kurmura*)
½ cup chopped onions
½ cup boiled, peeled and chopped potatoes
¼ cup Nylon *sev*, page 19
6 to 8 *papadis/puris*, crushed
4 tsp *masala dal*, page 23
4 tsp roasted peanuts

4 tsp roasted *chana* (whole Bengal gram)
4 tbsp *sukha teekha chutney*, recipe above
¾ tsp dry *masala* powder, page 22
1 tbsp lemon juice
Salt to taste
1 tbsp finely chopped raw mangoes (optional)
2 tbsp finely chopped coriander (*dhania*)

For the garnish
½ cup Nylon *sev*, page 19
4 tsp chopped coriander (*dhania*)

For serving
4 *papadis*

1. Combine all the ingredients in a large bowl and mix well.
2. Place equal portions of *bhel* on 4 plates and garnish each plate with 2 tbsp of *sev* and 1 tsp of coriander.
   Serve immediately with *papadis*.

SEV PURI

Let's call it the Indian canapé.! Tiny discs or flattened papadis serve as the base to hold an astounding topping of veggies and chutneys, garnished with sev! An appetiser that can steal the thunder out of any meal! What's more, you'll get a dish of around six puris for just Rs. 10 to 15.

Preparation Time: 10 minutes. **Cooking Time:** Nil. **Makes** 4 plates.

24 *papadis*
1 cup boiled, peeled and chopped potatoes
¾ cup finely chopped onions
¼ cup *geela lehsun ka chutney*, page 18
½ cup *teekha phudina chutney*, page 22
¾ cup *meetha chutney*, page 10
4 tsp dry *masala* powder, page 22
1 lemon, cut into halves
1 cup Nylon *sev*, page 19
½ cup finely chopped tomatoes
4 tsp finely chopped raw mangoes

For the garnish
4 tbsp chopped coriander *(dhania)*
4 tsp *masala dal*, page 23

1. Arrange 6 *papadis* on a plate and place ½ tbsp of potatoes and 2 tsp of onions over each *papadi*.
2. Top each *papadi* with ¼ tsp of *geela lehsun ka chutney*, ½ tsp *teekha phudina chutney* and ½ tbsp of *meetha chutney*.
3. Sprinkle 1 tsp of dry *masala* powder and squeeze some lemon juice evenly over the *papadis*.
4. Sprinkle ¼th of the *sev*, 2 tbsp of tomatoes and 1 tsp of raw mangoes evenly over the *papadis* and serve immediately garnished with 1 tbsp of coriander and 1 tsp of *masala dal*.
5. Repeat with the remaining ingredients to make 3 more plates.

RAGDA PATTICE

The very sight of the ragda, heaped upon a simmering thali surrounded by the ghee-roasted pattice, is enough to stir up your digestive enzymes! Place your order, and within a jiffy the vendor will get into action, placing steaming hot ragda in a plate, followed by the tasty pattice, chutneys, chopped onions, masala and coriander! Truly a meal in itself!

Preparation Time: 10 minutes. **Cooking Time:** 25 minutes. **Makes** 4 plates.
Soaking Time: Overnight.

For the *ragda*
¾ cup *safed vatana* (dried white peas)
½ tsp mustard seeds *(rai / sarson)*
A pinch asafoetida *(hing)*
¼ tsp turmeric powder *(haldi)*
Salt to taste

For the pattice
2 cups boiled, peeled and mashed potatoes
2 tsp cornflour
¼ tsp turmeric powder *(haldi)*
Salt to taste
1 tsp ginger-green chilli paste
2 tsp ghee for cooking

To be mixed into dry red *masala* (makes approx. ¹⁄₃ cup)
2 tbsp chilli powder
3 tbsp coriander *(dhania)* powder
1 tbsp black salt *(sanchal)*
1 tbsp salt

For serving
¾ cup *meetha chutney*, page 10
¹⁄₃ cup *teekha phudina chutney*, page 22
4 tsp *geela lehsun ka chutney*, page 18
1 tsp dry red *masala*, recipe above
8 tbsp Nylon *sev*, page 19
4 tbsp finely chopped onions
8 *papadis*, crushed

For the garnish
4 tsp finely chopped coriander *(dhania)*

For the *ragda*
1. Soak the *safed vatana* overnight or for atleast 6 to 8 hours.
2. Drain the *safed vatana*, add 2 cups of water and pressure cook for 5 to 6 whistles.
3. Allow the steam to escape before opening the lid.
4. Heat the oil in a *kadhai* and add the mustard seeds.
5. When the seeds crackle, add the asafoetida, turmeric powder, *vatana*, salt and 1 cup of water and mash the *vatana* slightly, using the back of a spoon.
6. Simmer for 8 to 10 minutes or till it thickens and keep aside.

For the pattice
1. Combine the potatoes, cornflour, turmeric powder and ginger-green chilli paste and salt in a bowl and mix well.
2. Divide the mixture into 8 equal portions and shape each portion into a flat round.
3. Cook each *pattice* on a *tava* (griddle) using ¼ tsp of ghee till they turn brown on both the sides. Keep aside.

How to serve
1. Place ¼th of the hot *ragda* on a plate, add 3 tbsp of *meetha chutney*, 1 tbsp of *teekha phudina chutney*, 1 tsp of *geela lehsun ka chutney* and ¼ tsp of dry red *masala* and mix lightly.
2. Flatten 2 pattice and place on the *ragda* mixture.
3. Sprinkle 2 tbsp of *sev*, 1 tbsp of onions, ¼th of the crushed *papadi* and serve immediately garnished with 1 tsp of coriander.
4. Repeat with the remaining ingredients to make 3 more plates.

6. Repeat with the remaining dough and filling to make 3 more *kachoris*.
7. Heat the oil in a *kadhai* and deep-fry the *kachoris* on a slow flame till they turn crisp and golden brown in colour from all the sides. (The *kachoris* should puff up like *puris*. It will take time to fry on a slow flame as the crust is thick and needs to be cooked) Keep aside to cool.

How to serve
1. Crack a small hole in the centre of a *kachori* and arrange on a plate.
2. Stuff with 1 tbsp of *moong* sprouts and top with ¼ cup of curds, 1 tbsp of *meetha chutney* and 1½ tsp of *teekha phudina chutney*.
3. Sprinkle 1 tbsp of *sev,* ¼ tsp of dry *masala* powder and 1 tsp of coriander evenly over it and serve immediately.
4. Repeat with the remaining ingredients to make 3 more plates.

Idlis & Dosas

The sizzling sound of water on the hot tava unfailingly lures you to the dosa stall! A freshly-prepared crisp and thin dosa with an interesting filling definitely kindles your appetite, if not fills your stomach. As people get busier they have little time on their hands for breakfast – naturally, this wholesome dish sees an ever-growing market! Whether it is the typical masala or a Schezuan filling with a tinge of China, the dosa carts offer an unending range of fillings!

The Mysore masala made on the cart is very different from what is offered in restaurants. It has a unique filling with grated beetroot, other veggies and spices, which makes for a meal in itself. The vendor's deft handling of the filling, the way he mashes it ensuring that he doesn't spill any of it or tear the dosa, is a delight to behold!

Not to forget the idlis and wadas, which are popular accompaniments especially in the morning hours! The coconut chutney, the red chutney made with red chillies and chana dal, as well as the sambhar gives us more reason to indulge in these dosas.

How easy on the pocket: Rs. 10 to Rs. 50 (depending on the kind of preparation)

A few areas you just can't afford to miss:

Khau Galli, Churchgate • Khau Galli, Vallabhbaug Lane at Ghatkopar • Prem Nagar, Borivali • Mithibai College • Kandivali Chowpatty, S. V. Road.

IDLI

An ideal breakfast option for the busy-bee! Served piping hot, usually in portions of three per plate, who can say no to these healthy, steamed idlis that are accompanied by delectable sambhar and two chutneys too?

Preparation Time: 35 minutes.   **Cooking Time:** 35 minutes.   **Makes** 4 plates.
Soaking Time: 3 hours.   **Fermenting Time:** Overnight.

For the *idli* batter
⅓ cup *urad dal* (split black gram)
¼ tsp fenugreek *(methi)* seeds
1 cup parboiled rice *(ukada chawal)*
Salt to taste

For the coconut *chutney* (makes approx. 1 cup)
3 tbsp freshly grated coconut
2 tbsp roasted *chana dal (daria)*
2 small green chillies, roughly chopped
1 tsp chopped ginger *(adrak)*
2 tbsp chopped coriander *(dhania)*
6 to 7 curry leaves *(kadi patta)*
Salt to taste
2 tsp oil
½ tsp mustard seeds *(rai / sarson)*
½ tsp *urad dal* (split black gram)
3 to 4 curry leaves *(kadi patta)*
1 small whole dry Kashmiri red chilli, broken into pieces
¼ tsp asafoetida *(hing)*

For the green garlic chutney (makes approx. 1 cup)
1¼ cups chopped coriander *(dhania)*
1½ tbsp sour curds *(khatta dahi)*
1½ tbsp roasted *chana dal (daria)*
1 to 2 small green chillies, roughly chopped
1 tsp chopped ginger *(adrak)*
1½ tsp chopped garlic *(lehsun)*
1 tbsp chopped spinach *(palak)*
Salt to taste

For the sambhar
¾ cup *toovar (arhar) dal*
½ tbsp *chana dal* (split Bengal gram)
¼ cup chopped bottle gourd *(doodhi / lauki)*
¼ cup chopped drumstick *(saragva/sajjan ki phali)*
¼ cup chopped red pumpkin *(kaddu)*
¼ cup shallots (Madras onions)
¼ cup chopped tomatoes
¾ tbsp tamarind *(imli)* pulp
Salt to taste
1 tbsp oil
½ tsp mustard seeds *(rai / sarson)*
¼ tsp fenugreek *(methi)* seeds
6 to 7 curry leaves *(kadi patta)*
¼ tsp asafoetida *(hing)*

Other ingredients
¼ tsp oil for greasing

For the *idli* batter
1. Soak the *urad dal* and fenugreek seeds in enough water for 3 hours, drain and blend in a mixer till smooth and frothy. Keep aside.
2. Soak the rice in enough water for 3 hours, drain and blend in a mixer to a coarse paste. Keep aside.
3. Combine the *urad dal* paste, rice paste and salt in a bowl and mix well.
4. Keep aside to ferment overnight.

For the coconut *chutney*
1. Combine the coconut, roasted *chana dal,* green chillies, ginger, coriander, curry leaves, salt and 3 tbsp of water and blend in a mixer to a smooth paste.
2. Transfer the paste to a bowl, add ⅓ cup of water and mix well.
3. For the tempering, heat the oil in a small pan and add the mustard seeds.
4. When the seeds crackle, add the *urad dal*, curry leaves, red chillies and asafoetida and sauté on a medium flame for a minute.

5. Pour this tempering over the *chutney* and mix well. Use as required and store remaining in an air-tight container in a deep-freezer.

For the green garlic *chutney*
1. Combine all the ingredients, add 2 tbsp of water and blend in a mixer till smooth.
2. Transfer to a bowl, add 1 cup of water and mix well. Use as required or store in an air-tight container in a deep-freezer.

For the *sambhar*
1. Clean, wash and soak the *dals* in water for 20 minutes. Drain.
2. Combine the *dals* and 1½ cups of water and pressure cook for 4 to 5 whistles.
3. Allow the steam to escape before opening the lid. Whisk it thoroughly and keep aside.
4. Combine the bottle gourd, drumstick, red pumpkin and 1 cup of water in a deep pan and cook on a medium flame for 10 to 12 minutes or till all the water has evaporated.
5. Add the cooked *dal*, onions, tomatoes, tamarind pulp, *sambhar masala*, salt and 3 cups of water, mix well and bring to boil.

6. For the tempering, heat the oil in a small pan and add the mustard seeds.
7. When the seeds crackle, add the fenugreek, curry leaves and asafoetida and sauté for a few seconds.
8. Pour this tempering over the boiling *sambhar*, mix well and simmer for another 5 to 7 minutes, stirring ocassionally.

How to proceed
1. Mix the fermented *idli* batter well and place spoonfuls of the batter into greased *idli* moulds and steam in a steamer for 8 to10 minutes.
2. Remove, cool for a few seconds and demould.
3. Place 3 *idlis* each on 4 plates and serve immediately with coconut *chutney*, green garlic *chutney* and *sambhar*.

Handy tip:

Since the rice and *urad dal* batter is ground separately, ensure that you mix well before fermenting. *Urad dal* tends to sink to the bottom and thus mixing is very important before and after fermenting.

35

SADA DOSA

Fffzzzzzzzzzzzzzzz! Your ear wakes up your gastronomic juices as soon as it hears the vendor sprinkling water on the hot tava. Enjoy the moment when he pours the batter and spreads it into a thin, crisp dosa, which is then rolled up and served along with sambhar and other chutneys.

Preparation Time: 20 minutes. **Cooking Time:** 15 to 20 minutes. **Makes** 4 plates.
Soaking Time: 3 to 4 hours. **Fermenting Time:** 6 to 8 hours.

For the *dosa* batter
1 cup raw short-grained rice *(chawal)* / parboiled rice *(ukada chawal)*
1/3 cup *urad dal* (split black gram)
5 to 7 fenugreek *(methi)* seeds
1 tbsp rice flakes *(poha)* (optional), soaked and drained
Salt to taste
1 tbsp *besan* (Bengal gram flour)

Other ingredients
1/4 tsp oil for greasing
4 tsp oil for cooking

For serving
Coconut *chutney,* page 34
Green garlic *chutney,* page 34
Sambhar, page 34

For the *dosa* batter (makes approx. 3 cups)
1. Clean, wash and soak the rice in enough water for atleast 3 to 4 hours.
2. Clean, wash and soak the *urad dal* and fenugreek seeds in enough water for atleast 3 to 4 hours.
3. Drain the rice, add the rice flakes, add a little water (approx. 1/4 cup of water) and blend in a mixer to a smooth paste.
4. Drain the *urad dal* and fenugreek seeds, add a little water (approx. 1 tbsp of water) and blend in a mixer to a smooth paste.
5. Combine the rice paste and *urad dal* paste, mix well and cover and allow it to ferment in a warm place for atleast 6 to 8 hours.
6. Add 1/2 cup of water, salt and *besan* and mix well.
7. Remove 1 cup of the prepared batter to make *dosas* and store the remaining batter in an air-tight container in a deep-freezer.

How to proceed
1. Pour 1/4th of the batter on the greased non-stick *tava* (griddle) (refer handy tip) and spread in a circular motion to make a 225 mm. (9") thin *dosa*.
2. Smear 1 tsp of oil over it and cook till the *dosa* turns brown in colour and crisp.
3. Fold over to make a cone, semi-circle or a roll.
4. Place the *dosa* on a plate and serve immediately with coconut *chutney*, green garlic *chutney* and *sambhar*.
5. Repeat with the remaining ingredients to make 3 more plates.

Handy tip:

Before making the *dosas* grease the non-stick *tava* (griddle) once with 1/4 tsp of oil and wipe with a slice of onion or potato. Sprinkle a little water on it (it should sizzle immediately) and wipe off using a piece of cloth. Alternatively, spread a portion of the batter to make a small sample *dosa*, cook it and discard. Follow these tips once, before making the *dosas* to ensure that the remaining *dosas* do not stick to the *tava* (griddle) and can be cooked easily.

VARIATIONS:
BUTTER SADA DOSA

Instead of using oil for cooking, smear 1 tbsp of butter over each *dosa* (at step no.2, page 36) and sprinkle ¼ tsp of *garam masala* evenly over it. Cook till the *dosa* turns crisp and brown in colour.

CHUTNEY BUTTER SADA DOSA

Like butter *sada dosa*, smear 1 tbsp of butter over the *dosa* and spread 2 tsp of green garlic *chutney*, page 34, evenly over it. Cook till the *dosa* turns crisp and brown in colour. As a Jain variation, use 2 tsp of green *chutney*, page 52, to make the same *dosa*.

PAV BHAJI DOSA

Vendors usually make the *pav bhaji* stuffing over the *dosa*, which is smeared on the *tava* (griddle). You can follow the same method of making the *bhaji* on the *dosa* (refer page 62 for the *Pav Bhaji* recipe) or you can make it in a *kadhai* and then smear it over the *dosas*. Smear approximately ⅓ cup of *bhaji* over a *dosa,* add 1 tbsp of butter and grated cheese over it if you like (at step no.2, page 36). Serve hot with coconut *chutney*, green garlic *chutney* and *sambhar*.

MASALA DOSA

A tried-and-tested recipe that serves as a wholesome answer to the hungry palate! A thin crisp dosa, engulfed in tempered potato bhaji, is folded up and neatly cut into four pieces. It's worth learning how the pieces are smoothly whisked onto the plate in one swift move once done!

Preparation Time: 20 minutes.   **Cooking Time:** 25 minutes.   **Makes** 4 plates.

For the *masala* (makes approx. 1⅓ cups)
1 tbsp oil
1 tsp mustard seeds *(rai/ sarson)*
1 tsp *chana dal* (split Bengal gram), soaked and drained
7 to 8 curry leaves *(kadi patta)*
1 tsp chopped green chillies
⅓ cup sliced onions
1¼ cups boiled, peeled and chopped potatoes
½ tsp turmeric powder *(haldi)*
Salt to taste
1 tbsp finely chopped coriander *(dhania)*

Other ingredients
1 cup *dosa* batter, page 36
4 tbsp butter for cooking
6 tbsp finely chopped onions
1 tsp *garam masala* (optional)

For serving
Coconut *chutney*, page 34
Green garlic *chutney*, page 34
Sambhar, page 34

For the *masala*
1. Heat the oil in a *kadhai* and add the mustard seeds.
2. When the seeds crackle, add the *chana dal* and sauté on a medium flame till the *dal* turns light brown in colour.
3. Add the curry leaves, green chillies and onions, mix well and sauté on a slow flame for 5 minutes, till the onions turn translucent.
4. Add the potatoes, turmeric powder, salt and coriander, mix well and cook on a medium flame for another minute, while stirring occasionally. Keep aside.

How to proceed
1. Pour ¼th of the *dosa* batter on the greased non-stick *tava* (griddle) (refer handy tip, page 36) and spread in a circular motion to make a 225 mm. (9") thin *dosa*.
2. Smear 1 tbsp of butter and spread ¼th of the *masala* evenly over the *dosa* using a spatula.
3. Sprinkle 1½ tbsp of onions and ¼ tsp of *garam masala* evenly over it and cook till the *dosa* turns brown in colour.
4. Fold over while pressing it lightly using spatula to make a flat roll and cut into 4 equal pieces using sharp edge of the spatula on the *tava* (griddle).
5. Place the pieces on a plate and serve immediately with coconut *chutney*, green garlic *chutney* and *sambhar*.
6. Repeat with the remaining ingredients to make 3 more plates.

MYSORE SADA DOSA

Hmmm, when you want to have a quick and light meal, but are in too perky a mood for sada dosa, then go for the Mysore sada dosa, which is not too heavy on the tummy but still has a nice, semi-spicy flavour, thanks to the Mysore chutney!

Preparation Time: 20 minutes.   **Cooking Time:** 15 minutes.   **Makes** 4 plates

For the Mysore *chutney* (makes approx. ¾ cup)
1 tbsp oil
2 tbsp *chana dal* (split Bengal gram)
½ tbsp *urad dal* (split black gram)
3 to 4 whole dry Kashmiri red chillies, broken into pieces
1 tsp chilli powder
2 tsp tamarind *(imli)* pulp
½ tsp black peppercorns *(kalimirch)*
1 tsp grated jaggery *(gur)*
⅓ cup freshly grated coconut
Salt to taste

Other ingredients
1 cup *dosa* batter, page 36
4 tbsp butter for cooking

For serving
Coconut *chutney*, page 34
Green garlic *chutney*, page 34
Sambhar, page 34

For the Mysore *chutney*
1. Heat the oil in a broad pan, add the *chana dal* and *urad dal* and sauté on a medium flame till they turn golden brown in colour.
2. Add the red chillies and sauté on a medium flame for 2 minutes.
3. Add the chilli powder, tamarind pulp, peppercorns, jaggery and coconut, mix well and sauté on a medium flame for a minute. Keep aside.
4. When cool, add the salt and blend in a mixer to a smooth paste, adding water as required. (This recipe requires 4 tbsp of the *chutney*, store the remaining in an air-tight container in a deep-freezer).

How to proceed
1. Pour ¼th of the *dosa* batter on the non-stick *tava* (griddle) (refer handy tip, page 36) and spread in a circular motion to make a 225 mm. (9") thin *dosa*.
2. Smear 1 tbsp of butter and 1 tbsp of the Mysore *chutney* evenly over the *dosa* using a spatula and cook till the *dosa* turns brown in colour and crisp.
3. Fold over to make a semi-circle or a roll.
4. Place it on a plate and serve immediately with coconut *chutney*, green garlic *chutney* and sambhar.
5. Repeat with the remaining ingredients to make 3 more plates.

MYSORE MASALA

Interestingly, Mumbai has mastered its own way of making Mysore masala dosa, which is quite different from the way it is actually made in Mysore! The innovation in Mumbai's streets is the addition of grated beetroot to the standard recipe! It's amazing how the vendor mashes up the mixture and cuts up the dosa without tearing the dosa or spilling the filling!

Preparation Time: 15 minutes. **Cooking Time:** 25 minutes. **Makes** 4 plates.

1 cup *dosa* batter, page 36
½ cup butter
4 tbsp chopped onions
4 tbsp shredded cabbage
1 cup chopped tomatoes
4 tbsp chopped capsicum
2 tbsp grated carrots
2 tbsp grated beetroot
4 tsp finely chopped coriander *(dhania)*
1 cup *masala*, page 38
8 tsp Mysore *chutney*, page 39
8 tsp green garlic *chutney*, page 34
2 tsp chilli powder
2 tsp *garam masala*
Salt to taste

For serving
Coconut *chutney*, page 34
Green garlic *chutney*, page 34
Sambhar, page 34

1. Pour ¼th of the *dosa* batter on the non-stick *tava* (griddle) (refer handy tip, page 36) and spread in a circular motion to make a 225 mm. (9") thin *dosa*.
2. Place 1 tbsp of butter in the centre, add 1 tbsp of onions, 1 tbsp of cabbage, ¼ cup of tomatoes, 1 tbsp of capsicum, ½ tbsp of carrots, ½ tbsp of beetroot, 1 tsp of coriander and 1 tbsp of water, mix well and cover and cook for a few seconds.
3. Add ¼ cup of *masala*, 2 tsp of Mysore *chutney*, 2 tsp of green garlic *chutney*, ½ tsp of chilli powder, ½ tsp of *garam masala* and salt, mix well and mash using a potato masher.
4. Add another ½ tbsp of butter, mix well and cover and cook for another minute.
5. Spread the filling evenly over the *dosa*, fold over while pressing it lightly using spatula to make a flat roll and cut into 4 equal pieces using sharp edge of the spatula on the *tava* (griddle).
6. Place the pieces on a plate and serve immediately with coconut *chutney*, green garlic *chutney* and *sambhar*.
7. Repeat with the remaining ingredients to make 3 more plates.

SCHEZUAN CHOPSUEY DOSA

Never thought South Indian food could do a waltz with Chinese cuisine? Check out the Chinese versions of dosas served on the streets of Mumbai before you decide! A hot favourite amongst teenagers, this combo of Schezuan sauce, noodles and veggies adds a new, young feel to the robust dosa!

Preparation Time: 15 minutes.   **Cooking Time:** 25 minutes.   **Makes** 4 plates.

1 cup dosa batter, page 36
4 tbsp butter
1 cup chopped onions
1 cup shredded cabbage
1 cup carrot juliennes
1 cup capsicum juliennes
Salt to taste
6 tbsp Schezuan sauce, page 72
8 tbsp tomato sauce
4 tsp chilli sauce
1 cup boiled noodles, page 73
8 tbsp finely chopped spring onion greens

For serving
Coconut *chutney*, page 34
Green garlic *chutney*, page 34
Sambhar, page 34

1. Pour ¼th of the *dosa* batter on the greased non stick *tava* (griddle) (refer handy tip, page 36) and spread in a circular motion to make a 225 mm. (9") thin *dosa*.
2. Place 1 tbsp of butter in the centre, add ¼ cup of onions, ¼ cup of cabbage, ¼ cup of carrots, ¼ cup of capsicum and salt, mix well and cover and cook 2 to 3 minutes.
3. Add 1½ tbsp of Schezuan sauce, 2 tbsp of tomato sauce, 1 tsp of chilli sauce, ¼ cup of noodles and 2 tbsp of spring onion greens, mix well and cover and cook for another 2 minutes.
4. Cook till the *dosa* turns brown in colour and crisp, fold over while pressing it lightly using spatula to make a roll and cut into 2 to 3 equal pieces using sharp edge of the spatula on the *tava* (griddle).
5. Place the pieces on a plate and serve immediately with coconut *chutney*, green garlic *chutney* and *sambhar*.
6. Repeat with the remaining ingredients to make 3 more plates.

VARIATION:
JAIN SCHEZUAN CHOPSUEY DOSA

To make the Jain version, follow the same recipe (as given above) but simply replace onions and spring onion greens with equal quantities of cabbage. For Jain Schezuan sauce, follow the Schezuan sauce recipe as given on page 72, but omit garlic and increase ginger to ⅓ cup.

SPRING DOSA

A tweaked version of the Schezuan dosa where the filling has the basic Chinese trio of vinegar, soya and chilli sauces! You could look at it as the Chinese 'sada dosa'! Hakka noodles and veggies form the bulk of this recipe.

Preparation Time: 15 minutes. **Cooking Time:** 25 minutes. **Makes** 4 plates.

1 cup *dosa* batter, page 36
4 tbsp butter
1 cup chopped onions
1 cup shredded cabbage
1 cup carrot juliennes
1 cup capsicum juliennes
Salt and freshly ground pepper to taste
4 tbsp tomato sauce
4 tsp chilli sauce
4 tsp soya sauce
2 tsp vinegar
1 cup boiled noodles, page 73
8 tbsp finely chopped spring onion greens

For serving
Coconut *chutney*, page 34
Green garlic *chutney*, page 34
Sambhar, page 34

1. Pour ¼th of the *dosa* batter on the greased non-stick *tava* (griddle) (refer handy tip, page 36) and spread in a circular motion to make a 225 mm. (9") thin *dosa*.
2. Place 1 tbsp of butter in the centre, add ¼ cup of onions, ¼ cup of cabbage, ¼ cup of carrots, ¼ cup of capsicum, salt and pepper, mix well and cover and cook for 2 minutes.

3. Add 1 tbsp of tomato sauce, 1 tsp of chilli sauce, 1 tsp of soya sauce, ½ tsp of vinegar, ¼ cup of noodles and 2 tbsp of spring onion greens, mix well and cover and cook for another minute.
4. Spread the stuffing evenly over the *dosa* using a spatula and cook till the *dosa* turns brown and crisp.
5. Fold over while pressing it lightly using spatula to make a flat roll and cut into 4 equal pieces using sharp edge of the spatula on the *tava* (griddle).
6. Place the pieces on a plate and serve immediately with coconut *chutney*, green garlic *chutney* and *sambhar*.
7. Repeat with the remaining ingredients to make 3 more plates.

VARIATION:
JAIN SPRING DOSA

To make the Jain version, follow the same recipe (as given above) but simply replace onions and spring onion greens with equal quantities of cabbage.

ONION UTTAPA

Uttapa deserves to be called the Indian pizza as it lends itself to several toppings, the most popular being crisp cooked onions. You may also try other combinations such as onion and tomatoes. Usually vendors spread the topping over the uttapa batter and press it in well with their wet fingers. But, to avoid hurting your fingers, use a spatula if you're a novice!

Preparation Time: 10 minutes.   **Cooking Time:** 25 minutes.   **Makes** 4 plates.

To be mixed together into a mixture
2 cups finely chopped onions
4 tsp finely chopped green chillies
4 tsp finely chopped coriander *(dhania)*
1 tsp *garam masala*
Salt to taste

Other ingredients
3 cups *dosa* batter, page 36
6 tbsp butter for cooking

For serving
Coconut *chutney*, page 34
Green garlic *chutney,* page 34
Sambhar, page 34

1. Pour ¾ cup of the *dosa* batter on the greased non-stick *tava* (griddle) (refer handy tip, page 36) and spread in a circular motion to make a 175 mm. (7") thick *uttapa* and cook on a medium flame for a minute.
2. Spread ¼th of the mixture evenly over it and press it lightly using a spatula.
3. Place 1 tbsp of butter in the centre, smear evenly over it using a spatula and cook for 2 minutes.
4. Turn over and cook on the other side till it turns light brown in colour.
5. Smear another ½ tbsp of butter evenly over it and cut into 4 equal pieces using the sharp edge of the spatula on the *tava* (griddle).
6. Place the pieces on a plate and serve immediately with coconut *chutney,* green garlic *chutney* and *sambhar.*
7. Repeat with the remaining ingredients to make 3 more plates.

VARIATION:
TOMATO CAPSICUM UTTAPA

Those who do not like onions can make this variant by replacing onions with 1 cup each of sliced tomatoes and capsicum in the mixture and proceed as per the recipe.

47

SANDWICH UTTAPA

An uttapa with a difference! The spread-out batter is topped with veggies and coated with another layer of batter, to make a sandwich, which is then cut into equal wedges and served hot with the typical south Indian accompaniments.

Preparation Time: 15 minutes.   **Cooking Time:** 35 minutes.   **Makes** 4 plates.

4 cups *dosa* batter, page 36
6 tbsp green garlic *chutney*, page 34
6 tbsp coconut chutney, page 34
1 cup finely chopped onions
1 cup finely chopped tomatoes
½ cup chopped capsicum
4 tsp chilli powder
2 tsp *garam masala*
Salt to taste
4 tbsp butter for cooking

For serving
Coconut *chutney*, page 34
Green garlic *chutney*, page 34
Sambhar, page 34

1. Pour ¾ cup of the *dosa* batter on the greased non-stick *tava* (griddle) (refer handy tip, page 36) and spread in a circular motion to make a 175 mm. (7") thick *uttapa*.

2. Place ½ tbsp of butter in the centre, add 1½ tbsp of green garlic *chutney*, 1½ tbsp of coconut *chutney*, mix well and smear evenly over the *uttapa* using a spatula.
3. Spread ¼ cup of onions, ¼ cup of tomatoes, 2 tbsp of capsicum, 1 tsp of chilli powder, ½ tsp of *garam masala* and salt evenly over the *uttapa* and press it lightly, using a spatula.
4. Pour ¼ cup of batter over the vegetables, spread it evenly using spatula to make a thin layer, turn over and cook for 3 to 4 minutes.
5. Smear another ½ tbsp of butter evenly over it and cut into 4 equal pieces using the sharp edge of the spatula on the *tava* (griddle).
6. Place the pieces on a plate and serve immediately with coconut *chutney*, green garlic *chutney* and *sambhar*.
7. Repeat with the remaining ingredients to make 3 more plates.

MEDU WADA

This south Indian delicacy has become an integral part of Mumbai's street food. No dosa stall is complete without piping hot deep-fried wadas. Just ask, and can get them submerged in sambhar. The idli-wada combination is a favourite for breakfast!

Preparation Time: 15 minutes. **Cooking Time:** 30 minutes. **Makes** 4 plates.
Soaking Time: 2 hours.

1 cup *urad dal* (split black gram)
5 to 6 black peppercorns *(kalimirch)*
8 to 10 curry leaves *(kadi patta)*
1 tsp roughly chopped ginger *(adrak)*
1 tsp finely chopped green chillies
Salt to taste
Oil for deep-frying

For serving
Coconut *chutney,* page 34
Green garlic *chutney,* page 34
Sambhar, page 34

1. Clean, wash and soak the *urad dal* in enough water for atleast 2 hours.
2. Drain, add the peppercorns, curry leaves and ginger and blend in a mixer to a smooth batter, adding little water.
3. Add the green chillies and salt, mix well and keep aside.
4. Wet your fingers, take some batter and make a hole in the centre using your thumb.
5. Slip the *wada* gently into the hot oil and deep-fry on a medium flame till it turns golden brown in colour from all the sides.
6. Repeat with the remaining batter to make 7 more *medu wadas.* Drain on absorbent paper.
7. Place 2 *wadas* on a plate and serve immediately with coconut *chutney*, green garlic *chutney* and *sambhar.*
8. Repeat with the remaining ingredients to make 3 more plates.

Sandwiches

Vendors in mini carts (actually, you can't even call them carts) keep constantly applying butter and chutney to bread slices. A whole pack of bread is over in less than 10 minutes! The sandwich wala is always busy making different varieties of sandwiches. Since it is filling and cheap, it is extremely popular among Mumbaikars. A small stove and hand-toaster keeps popping out hot toasts, judiciously cut into four triangles, smeared with oodles of butter and served with chutney and ketchup. Those who do not prefer the crispy delights can go for an array of sandwiches with veggies, or just plain cheese and chillies, etc.

If you feel a spicy after-taste once digged into this delight, don't be embarrassed to ask for a slice of potato or cucumber as a freebie! The vendors give these away quite happily! Else, you could grab a bread butter aloo slice - potato slices placed between a bread slice - and munch on it till the spicy after-taste disappears. These days, vendors who can afford an automatic grill also dish out piping hot grilled sandwiches with a host of fillings.

How easy on the pocket: Rs. 10 to Rs. 40

A few areas you just can't afford to miss:

Swati Sandwich, Santa Cruz West ●
Jai Sandwich, National College, Bandra
● Mithibai College ● Passport Office
● Jaishree Sandwich Wala, Ghatkopar East
● Jalaram Sandwich, Ghatkopar East.

VEGETABLE SANDWICH

Common fare on the Mumbai streets, this is a wholesome meal that you can feast on however short of time you are! Each sandwich is neatly cut into six equal pieces and served with tomato ketchup and chutney. And not to worry if you like it piping hot… bhaiyya will be very happy to toast them for you.

Preparation Time: 15 minutes. **Cooking Time:** A few seconds. **Makes** 4 plates.

To be blended into green *chutney* (makes approx. ¾ cup)
1 cup roughly chopped coriander *(dhania)*
¼ cup chopped spinach *(palak)*
1½ slices bread
6 to 7 green chillies
Salt to taste
½ tsp lemon juice
2 to 3 tbsp water

For the sandwich *masala* (makes approx. ¾ cup)
½ cup cumin seeds *(jeera)*
2 tsp cloves *(laung / lavang)*
2 tsp cinnamon *(dalchini)*
4 tsp black peppercorns *(kalimirch)*
4 tsp fennel seeds *(saunf)*
4 tsp black salt *(sanchal)*
2 tsp dry mango powder *(amchur)*

Other ingredients
8 slices bread
8 tsp butter
4 tsp green *chutney*, recipe above
2 medium sized cucumber, peeled and cut into thin slices
3 tsp sandwich *masala,* recipe above
1 medium sized onion, peeled and cut into thin slices
3 medium sized potatoes, boiled, peeled and cut into slices
1 small beetroot, boiled, peeled and cut into thin slices
3 medium sized tomatoes, cut into thin slices

For serving
2 tsp butter
Tomato ketchup
Green *chutney*, recipe above

For the sandwich *masala*
1. Dry roast the cumin seeds on a *tava* (griddle) for a few seconds, while stirring continuously and keep aside to cool.
2. Combine all the ingredients including the roasted cumin seeds and blend in a mixer to a fine powder.
3. Use as required and store remaining in an air-tight container.

How to proceed
1. Trim off the edges of the bread slices, apply 1 tsp of butter and ½ tsp of green *chutney* on each slice and keep aside.
2. Place a slice of bread, with the buttered side facing upwards, on a clean flat surface.
3. Arrange a few cucumber slices (approx. 8 to 10) and sprinkle ¼ tsp of sandwich *masala* evenly over it.
4. Arrange 2 onion slices, 4 to 5 potato slices and sprinkle ¼ tsp of sandwich *masala* evenly over it.
5. Arrange 2 beetroot slices, 6 to 7 tomato slices and sprinkle ¼ tsp of sandwich *masala* evenly over it.
6. Top with another slice of bread, with the buttered side facing downwards and press it lightly.
7. Cut into 6 equal pieces, place them on a plate and apply ½ tsp of butter evenly over it.
8. Serve immediately with tomato ketchup and green *chutney.*
9. Repeat with the remaining ingredients to make 3 more plates.

VARIATIONS:

BROWN BREAD VEGETABLE SANDWICH

Replace white bread in the recipe, page 52 with brown bread for a healthier version of this delicacy.

CHEESE VEGETABLE SANDWICH

Simply grate a generous amount of cheese over the tomatoes (after step no.5 in the recipe, page 52), top with another slice of bread and grate some more cheese over it. Cut into 6 equal pieces and serve immediately.

VEGETABLE TOAST SANDWICH

Place a vegetable sandwich, page 52 in an electric toaster or a hand toaster and cook using butter till it turns brown and crisp on both sides. Remove and cut into 6 equal pieces and serve hot topped with butter and Nylon *sev*, page 19.

JAIN VEGETABLE SANDWICH

To make a Jain version, use generous amounts of cucumber and tomatoes in the recipe given on page 52. Do not add onions, potatoes and beetroot. You can have this sandwich as is or toasted.

MASALA TOAST

The humble potato comes to the rescue once again, to calm your hunger pangs! The unique stove and toaster used to make these toasts is a typical trademark of street-side food. Mind not the prodigal portions of butter used to ensure even grilling of the toast! Forget the calories and relish this piping hot, topped with crunchy sev.

Preparation Time: 15 minutes. **Cooking Time:** 20 minutes. **Makes** 4 plates.

To be blended into garlic green *chutney* (makes approx. ¾ cup)
1½ cups roughly chopped coriander (*dhania*)
¼ cup freshly grated coconut
1 tbsp chopped spinach (*palak*)
1 tbsp roughly chopped garlic (*lehsun*)
6 to 7 green chillies
Salt to taste
A few drops of lemon juice
2 to 3 tbsp water

For the *aloo masala*
2 tsp oil
½ tsp mustard seeds (*rai/ sarson*)
6 to 8 curry leaves (*kadi patta*)
1 cup boiled, peeled and roughly mashed potatoes
1 tbsp soaked and boiled *hara vatana* (dried green peas) or boiled fresh green peas
¼ tsp turmeric powder (*haldi*)
1 tsp ginger-green chilli paste
1 tbsp finely chopped coriander (*dhania*)
Salt to taste

Other ingredients
8 slices bread
8 tsp butter
4 tsp green *chutney*, page 52
1 medium sized cucumber, peeled and cut into thin slices or 1 cup shredded cabbage
2 tsp sandwich *masala*, page 52
1 medium sized onion, peeled and cut into thin slices
1 medium sized tomato, cut into thin slices
1 small capsicum, deseeded and thinly sliced
4½ tsp butter for greasing and cooking

For serving
2 tsp butter
4 tbsp Nylon *sev*, page 19
Tomato ketchup
Garlic green *chutney*, recipe besides

For the *aloo masala*
1. Heat the oil in a small *kadhai* and add the mustard seeds.
2. When the seeds crackle, add the curry leaves and sauté on a medium flame for a few seconds.
3. Add the potatoes, *hara vatana,* turmeric powder, ginger-green chilli paste, coriander and salt, mix well and cook on a medium flame for another minute. Remove from the flame and keep aside to cool.

How to proceed
1. Trim off the edges of the bread slices, apply 1 tsp of butter and ½ tsp of green *chutney* on each slice and keep aside.
2. Place a slice of bread, with the buttered side facing upwards, on a clean flat surface.
3. Arrange a few cucumber slices (approx. 6 to 7) or ¼ cup of shredded cabbage and sprinkle ¼ tsp of sandwich *masala* evenly over it.
4. Place ¼th of the *aloo masala* and spread evenly over it.
5. Arrange 2 onion slices, 2 tomato slices and 2 capsicum slices over the *aloo masala* and sprinkle ¼ tsp of sandwich *masala* evenly over it.
6. Top with another slice of bread, with the buttered side facing downwards and press it lightly.
7. Place it in a greased sandwich toaster and cook using 1 tsp of butter, till it turns brown and crisp on both the sides. (Refer handy tip, page 55).

8. Cut into 6 equal pieces, place it on a plate and apply ½ tsp of butter evenly over it.
9. Sprinkle 1 tbsp of *sev* evenly over it and serve immediately with tomato ketchup and garlic green *chutney*.
10. Repeat with the remaining ingredients to make 3 more plates.

Handy tip:

Vendors use a hand toaster to toast the sandwich over the stove on the roadside. While using a hand toaster, pre-heat the toaster over the flame, apply some butter and then place the sandwich inside. Cook it on one side till it turns brown. Turn the toaster and cook till the sandwich turns brown on the other side.

VARIATION:
CHEESE MASALA TOAST

Grate a generous amount of cheese over the capsicum slices (after step no.5, page 54), top with another slice of bread. Cook in a sandwich toaster and cut into 6 equal pieces. Grate some more cheese over the pieces and serve immediately.

VEGETABLE GRILL SANDWICH

One sandwich is definitely enough to feed two hungry mouths! What more can you ask for than a double-decker sandwich made of three triangular slices of bread piled with veggies? Stalls near colleges grill at least 15 to 20 sandwiches before the lunch break, and they vanish within seconds.!

Preparation Time: 25 minutes. **Cooking Time:** 30 minutes. **Makes** 4 plates.

12 big slices bread (triangular in shape)
4 tbsp butter
2 tbsp green *chutney,* page 52
4 small cucumber, peeled and sliced
4 tsp sandwich *masala*, page 52
4 medium sized potatoes, boiled and peeled
2 medium sized onions, peeled and cut into thin slices
4 medium sized capsicum, deseeded and thinly sliced
6 medium sized tomatoes, cut into thin slices
8 tsp butter for greasing and cooking

For serving
4 tsp butter
Tomato ketchup
Green *chutney,* page 52

1. Apply 1 tsp of butter and ½ tsp of green *chutney* on each slice and keep aside.
2. Place a slice of bread, with the buttered side facing upwards, on a clean flat surface.
3. Arrange ½ of the cucumber slices and sprinkle ¼ tsp of sandwich *masala* evenly over it.
4. Grate a potato evenly and sprinkle ¼ tsp of sandwich *masala* evenly over it.
5. Arrange ½ of the onion slices and sprinkle ¼ tsp of sandwich *masala* evenly over it.
6. Place another slice of bread with the buttered side facing downwads and arrange ½ of the capsicum slices and ½ of the tomato slices evenly over it.

7. Sprinkle ¼ tsp of sandwich *masala* evenly over it and top with one more slice of bread with the buttered side facing downwards and press it lightly.
8. Place it in a greased grill sandwich toaster and cook using 2 tsp of butter, till it turns brown and crisp on both the sides.
9. Remove and cut into 8 pieces, place it on a plate and apply ½ tsp of butter evenly over it.
10. Serve immediately with tomato ketchup and green *chutney.*
11. Repeat with the remaining ingredients to make 3 more plates.

VARIATIONS:

CHEESE/ PANEER GRILL SANDWICH

Simply grate ½ cup of cheese/ *paneer* over the onion slices (after step 5 in the above recipe) and follow the remaining procedure as above. Just before serving, grate some more cheese/ *paneer* over the pieces and serve immediately.

JAIN VEGETABLE GRILL SANDWICH

To make a Jain version, replace onions and potatoes with generous amounts of cucumber and tomatoes in the above recipe.

CHEESE CHILLY TOAST

A roadside version of the authentic cheese chilli toast, this is not an open sandwich which is gratinated but a stuffed version of the same. Stuffed with oodles of cheese and green chillies, this is a rare treat that is slowly gaining popularity in street-side sandwich corners. This recipe is one of the many variants of the chilli cheese toast.

Preparation Time: 10 minutes.   **Cooking Time:** 15 minutes.   **Makes** 4 plates.

8 slices bread
8 tsp butter
4 tsp green *chutney,* page 52
1⅓ cups grated cooking cheese
1 tsp finely chopped green chillies
1 tsp sandwich *masala,* page 52
4½ tsp butter for greasing and cooking

For serving
2 tsp butter
Tomato ketchup
Green chutney, page 52

1. Trim off the edges of the bread slices, apply 1 tsp of butter and ½ tsp of green *chutney* on each slice and keep aside.
2. Place a slice of bread, with the buttered side facing upwards, on a clean flat surface.
3. Spread ⅓ cup of cheese and sprinkle ¼ tsp of green chillies and ¼ tsp of sandwich *masala* evenly over it.
4. Top with another slice of bread, with the buttered side facing downwards and press it lightly
5. Place it in a greased sandwich toaster and cook using 1 tsp of butter, till it turns brown and crisp on both the sides. (Refer handy tip, page 55).
6. Cut diagonally into 4 equal pieces, place it on a plate and apply ½ tsp of butter evenly over it.
7. Serve immediately with tomato ketchup and green *chutney.*
8. Repeat with the remaining ingredients to make 3 more plates.

VARIATION:

You can add chopped onions and capsicum along with cheese and green chillies.

SAMOSA SANDWICH

The friendly samosa strikes a good chord anywhere whether with the humble pav or stuffed between bread slices! This rare combination is quite popular in certain localities in south Mumbai.

Preparation Time: 15 minutes.   **Cooking Time:** 15 to 20 minutes.   **Makes** 4 plates.

8 slices bread
8 tsp butter
4 tsp garlic green *chutney,* page 54 / green *chutney,* page 52
4 *samosas,* page 12
1 medium sized onion, peeled and cut into thin slices
1 small capsicum, deseeded and thinly sliced
1 tsp sandwich *masala,* page 52
4½ tsp butter for greasing and cooking

For serving
2 tsp butter
Tomato ketchup
Chilli sauce/ green *chutney,* page 52

1. Trim off the edges of the bread slices, apply 1 tsp of butter and ½ tsp of *chutney* on each slice and keep aside.

2. Place a slice of bread, with the buttered side facing upwards, on a clean flat surface.
3. Flatten a *samosa,* place it on the bread and arrange 2 to 3 onion slices and 2 capsicum slices over the *samosa.*
4. Sprinkle ¼ tsp of sandwich *masala* evenly over it and top with another slice of bread with the buttered side facing downwards and press it lightly.
5. Place it in a greased sandwich toaster and cook using 1 tsp of butter, till it turns brown and crisp on both the sides (refer handy tip, page 55).
6. Remove and cut into 6 equal pieces, place it on a plate and apply ½ tsp of butter evenly over it.
7. Serve immediately with tomato ketchup and chilli sauce / green *chutney.*
8. Repeat with the remaining ingredients to make 3 more plates.

Pav Bhaji

It is tough to cross a pav bhaji stall without succumbing to the temptation! Undeniably the most liked tava food - pav bhaji, served with onions, lemon and oodles of butter, is one food which even calorie-conscious people should dig into occasionally, to take a break.

A mélange of vegetables, sautéed and cooked in butter emit an intoxicating aroma, all thanks to the secret ingredient pav bhaji masala. Either you take the effort to dip the pieces of pav in the bhaji before relishing each piece, or you can have it 'sandwiched' between the pav and cooked. This is also commonly called masala pav. A small part of the pav bhaji wala's tava is dedicated to tava pulao, which is made in a jiffy with cooked rice, pav bhaji masala and vegetables.

Both the bhaji and the tava pulao are made in bulk and kept. When orders come flooding in, the vendor portions it out, does some last minute cooking and serves it piping hot. Those who enjoy pav bhaji extra spicy can ask for 'chutney fry', with its characteristic fiery feel! And last but not the least, for those who avoid onions and garlic, do try the Jain version of this delicacy. Didn't I tell you that Mumbai's streets have something for everybody!

How easy on the pocket: Rs. 15 to Rs. 45

A few areas you just can't afford to miss:

Khau Galli, Churchgate • Khau Galli, Vallabhbaug Lane Extension at Ghatkopar • Maruti Pav Bhaji Wala - Bajaj Road, Parle • Juhu Beach • Kandivali Chowpatty, S. V. Road.

PAV BHAJI

Pav bhaji is more than a mere snack! It's a quick meal that can be grabbed on the go since large potions of the bhaji are made in advance and simply reheated with a few spices before serving. You just need to wait till the pav is toasted to perfection with oodles of butter! Hmm, top with the raw onions, squeeze a tad of lemon atop the bhaji, and forget yourself!

Preparation Time: 20 minutes. **Cooking Time:** 30 minutes. **Makes** 4 plates.
Soaking time: 1 hour.

For the chilli-garlic paste (makes approx. ½ cup)
10 to 12 whole dry Kashmiri red chillies, deseeded
8 to 10 cloves garlic *(lehsun),* roughly chopped

For the *bhaji*
1 tbsp oil
2 tbsp butter
1 tbsp cumin seeds *(jeera)*
½ cup chopped capsicum
¾ cup finely chopped onions
1½ cups finely chopped tomatoes
2 tsp chilli powder
1½ tbsp *pav bhaji masala,* refer handy tip, page 63
Salt to taste
1½ cups boiled, peeled and mashed potatoes
¼ cup *hara vatana* (dry green peas), soaked, boiled and mashed
½ cup fresh green peas, boiled and lightly mashed
2 tbsp finely chopped coriander *(dhania)*

For the *pav*
8 *laddi pav*
8 tsp butter for cooking
1 tsp *pav bhaji masala*

For serving
1 cup finely chopped onions
4 lemon wedges
4 roasted *papads*
4 tsp butter

For the garnish
4 tbsp finely chopped coriander *(dhania)*

For the chilli-garlic paste
1. Soak the red chillies in enough warm water for atleast an hour.
2. Drain the chillies, add the garlic and blend in a mixer till smooth, adding enough water. Use as required and store remaining in an air-tight container in the deep-freezer.

For the *bhaji*
1. Heat the oil and 1 tbsp of butter on a large *tava* (griddle) or in a *kadhai* and add the cumin seeds.
2. When the seeds crackle, add 2 tbsp of chilli-garlic paste and sauté on a medium flame for a few seconds.
3. Add the capsicum and sauté on a medium flame for a minute.
4. Add the onions and sauté on a medium flame for 8 to 10 minutes.
5. Add the tomatoes, chilli powder, *pav bhaji masala,* salt and ½ cup of water, mix well and cook on a medium flame for 5 to 7 minutes or till the oil separates, while mashing continuously using a potato masher.
6. Add the potatoes, *hara vatana,* green peas, coriander, ⅓ cup of water and remaining 1 tbsp of butter and mash well using a potato masher and cook on a medium flame for 5 to 7 minutes, while stirring continuously.

For the *pav*
1. Slit 2 *pav* vertically and keep aside.
2. Heat a large *tava* (griddle), add 2 tsp of butter and ¼ tsp of *pav bhaji masala,* mix well and slit open the *pav* and place on it.
3. Cook on a medium flame till they turn light brown and crisp on both the sides. (add more butter if required).

How to serve

1. Place ¼th of hot *bhaji*, 2 *pav*, ¼ cup of onions, a lemon wedge and a *papad* on a plate.
2. Top the *bhaji* with 1 tsp of butter and serve immediately garnished with 1 tsp of coriander.
3. Repeat with the remaining ingredients to make 3 more plates.

Handy tip:

Pav bhaji masala is a spice blend, which is readily available under different brand names at most grocery stores.

VARIATIONS:
CHEESE PAV BHAJI

Add lots of grated cheese to the prepared *pav bhaji* and serve immediately.

KHADA PAV BHAJI

Serve *pav bhaji* in a different style! Don't worry, it does not involve any special method… it's just the way ingredients are chopped. *'Khada'* means whole. So, to make *khada pav bhaji,* follow the same recipe on page 62, but chop all the ingredients into cubes. Do not mash the *bhaji.*

JAIN PAV BHAJI

There is something for everybody on the streets of Mumbai. Those who do not eat potatoes, onions and garlic do not have to go home hungry! Pav bhaji is made for Jains using mashed peas and tomatoes.

Preparation Time: 20 minutes.   **Cooking Time:** 20 minutes.   **Makes** 4 plates.

To be blended into a red chilli paste (makes approx. 1½ cups)
35 to 40 whole dry Kashmiri red chillies, deseeded and soaked in ⅓ cup warm water

For the *bhaji*
1 tbsp oil
2 tbsp butter
1 tbsp cumin seeds *(jeera)*
½ cup chopped capsicum
3 cups finely chopped tomatoes
2 tsp chilli powder
1½ tbsp *pav bhaji masala,* refer handy tip
Salt to taste
¾ cup boiled cauliflower florets
⅓ cup *hara vatana* (dry green peas), soaked, boiled and mashed
¾ cup boiled green peas
2 tbsp finely chopped coriander *(dhania)*

For the *pav*
8 *laddi pav*
8 tsp butter for cooking
1 tsp *pav bhaji masala*

For the garnish
1 tbsp chopped coriander *(dhania)*

For serving
A few tomatoes slices
4 lemon wedges
4 roasted *papads*
4 tsp butter

For the *bhaji*
1. Heat the oil and butter on a large *tava* (griddle) or in a *kadhai* and add the cumin seeds.
2. When the seeds crackle, add 2 tbsp of red chilli paste and sauté on a medium flame for a few seconds.
3. Add the capsicum and sauté on a medium flame for a minute.
4. Add the tomatoes, chilli powder, *pav bhaji masala,* salt and ½ cup of water, mix well and cook on a medium flame for 5 to 7 minutes or till the oil separates, while mashing continuously using a potato masher.

5. Add the cauliflower, mashed *hara vatana*, green peas, coriander and ⅓ cup of water, mash well using a potato masher and cook on a medium flame for 5 to 7 minutes, while stirring continuously.

For the *pav*
1. Slit 2 *pav* vertically and keep aside.
2. Heat a large *tava* (griddle), add 2 tsp of butter and ¼ tsp of *pav bhaji masala*, mix well and slit open the *pav* and place on it.

3. Cook on a medium flame till they turn light brown and crisp on both the sides. (Add more butter if required).

How to serve
1. Place ¼th of the *bhaji*, 2 *pav*, a few tomato slices, a lemon wedge and a *papad* on a plate.
2. Top the *bhaji* with 1 tsp of butter and serve immediately garnished with coriander.
3. Repeat with the remaining ingredients to make 3 more plates.

MASALA PAV

Whoever invented bread will be awe-struck to see it being put to such good use! Quick and easy, masala pav is made by stuffing a spicy tomato-onion gravy inside butter-laden pavs. Sometimes, the pav is just roasted on the tava with butter, loads of coriander and pav bhaji masala. Ask for cheese along with it for a richer feel.

Preparation Time: 15 minutes. **Cooking Time:** 25 to 30 minutes. **Makes** 4 plates.

For the *masala*
4 tbsp butter
4 tsp cumin seeds *(jeera)*
4 tbsp chilli-garlic paste, page 62
1⅓ cups finely chopped onions
1 cup chopped capsicum
5 cups finely chopped tomatoes
Salt to taste
4 tsp chilli powder
8 tsp *pav bhaji masala,* page 63
2 tbsp finely chopped coriander *(dhania)*

Other ingredients
8 tsp butter
8 *laddi pav*

For the garnish
2 tbsp finely chopped coriander *(dhania)*

For serving
4 lemon wedges

For the *masala*
1. Heat the butter in a *kadhai* and add the cumin seeds.
2. When the seeds crackle, add the chilli-garlic paste, onions and capsicum, mix well and saute on a medium flame for 8 to 10 minutes or till the onions turn translucent, while stirring continuously.

3. Add the tomatoes, salt, chilli powder, *pav bhaji masala* and 1 cup of water, mix well and cover and cook on a medium flame for 10 to 12 minutes, stirring once in between.
4. Mash it lightly, add the coriander and simmer for another minute. Keep aside.

How to proceed
1. Heat 1 tsp of butter on a *tava* (griddle), add ¼th of the prepared *masala* and sauté on a medium flame for a few seconds.
2. Slit 2 *pav* vertically, open and place them on the *masala.*
3. Spread the *masala* evenly over the *pav* till they get evenly coated form all the sides.
4. Add another 1 tsp of butter and cook the *pav* on a medium flame for a few seconds.
5. Place the *masala pav* and a lemon wedge on a plate and serve immediately garnished with ½ tbsp of coriander and a lemon wedge.
6. Repeat with the remaining ingredients to make 3 more plates.

TAVA PULAO

Another quick treat off the pav bhaji cart! This delicious pulao is prepared in advance by the vendor, and shares a place on the pav bhaji tava. It is swiftly portioned out onto serving plates when the orders flow in, to appease the severest of hunger shots.

Preparation Time: 10 minutes. **Cooking Time:** 10 minutes. **Makes** 4 plates.

3 tbsp butter
2 tsp cumin seeds *(jeera)*
1½ tbsp chilli-garlic paste, page 62
½ cup finely chopped onions
½ cup chopped capsicum
1¼ cups finely chopped tomatoes
Salt to taste
¼ tsp turmeric powder *(haldi)*
2 tsp chilli powder
4 tsp *pav bhaji masala*, page 63
2½ cups cooked rice
¼ cup boiled fresh green peas
1 tbsp finely chopped coriander *(dhania)*

To be mixed into a *raita*
¾ cup fresh curds *(dahi)*, beaten
½ cup chopped onions
½ tsp finely chopped green chillies
1 tbsp finely chopped coriander *(dhania)*
Salt to taste

For serving
Raita, recipe above
4 roasted *papads*

1. Heat the butter on a large *tava* (griddle), add the cumin seeds and sauté on a medium flame till they crackle.
2. Add the chilli-garlic paste and onions, mix well and sauté on a medium flame for 3 to 4 minutes.
3. Add the capsicum, tomatoes, salt, turmeric powder, chilli powder, *pav bhaji masala* and ¼ cup of water, mix well and cook on a medium flame for 4 to 5 minutes or till the butter separates, stirring once in between.
4. Add the rice, green peas and coriander, toss gently and cook on a medium flame for another minute.
5. Place equal portions of *pulao* on 4 plates and serve immediately with *raita* and *papads*.

VARIATION:
JAIN TAVA PULAO

Replace chilli-garlic paste with red chilli paste, page 63, avoid adding onions and proceed as per the recipe.

PAV SANDWICH

There are times when you want to steer clear of high-calorie butter delights, although you are ravenously hungry! Those strange times when you think a sandwich will be the best thing, though it might still leave a little room in the tummy! This stouter brother of the humble sandwich might be just what you need -- try this rare snack of laadi pav flavoured and roasted on the tava and stuffed with basic sandwich fillings.

Preparation Time: 10 minutes. **Cooking Time:** 15 minutes. **Makes** 4 plates.

4 *laddi pav*
6 tbsp butter
¼ cup chilli-garlic paste, page 62
1 medium sized onion, peeled and cut into thin slices
3 medium sized potatoes, boiled, peeled and cut into slices
2 medium sized tomatoes, cut into thin slices
Salt to taste

1. Slit each *pav* vertically and keep aside.
2. Heat 1 tbsp of butter on a *tava* (griddle), add 1 tbsp of chilli-garlic paste and sauté on a medium flame for a second.
3. Place the *pav* on it and turn immediately on the other side so that it gets evenly coated from both the sides.
4. Open the *pav* and place it downwards on *tava* (griddle), add another ½ tbsp of butter and cook the *pav* on a medium flame for a minute, while moving it on *tava*.
5. Remove on clean, dry surface and arrange 2 to 3 onion slices, 4 to 5 potato slices and 4 to 5 tomato slices on the lower inside portion of the *pav*.
6. Sprinkle some salt evenly over the vegetables, close the upper portion of the *pav* and press it gently.
7. Place the *pav* sandwich on a plate, cut it diagonally into 2 equal pieces and serve immediately.
8. Repeat with the remaining ingredients to make 3 more plates.

Chinese

Once a preserve of elite restaurants, Chinese food has now become so popular that its influence has extended to street food too! Systematically assembled with all the necessary ingredients, the Chinese Cart is always on high flame, in the remotest of Mumbai's gallis. Each Chinese cart typically has a Chinese sounding name with a dragon sketched on the cart!

The pre-preps are all done meticulously – the neatly cut juliennes, cooked rice and noodles are all ready to go into the huge wok when the orders come pouring in. Chinese meals come in decent proportions and are evenly priced. Soups are served hot with crispy noodles and accompaniments. It is a delight to watch the way the vendor works his way with the wok, later portioning out the delights precisely into the plates.

All the dishes are made to suit the Indian palette and thus you will find it a little spicier and more coloured than the authentic Chinese fare. Another aspect worth noting is that the plates in which the Chinese meals are served are typically orange or brown in colour – this seems to have become an unwritten standard followed by most vendors!

How easy on the pocket: Rs. 15 to Rs. 60

A few areas you just can't afford to miss:

Chandavarkar Lane, Borivali • Khau Galli, Churchgate • Dumplings - Portuguese Church, Dadar • Kandivali Chowpatty, S. V. Road.

MANCHOW SOUP

An all-time favourite, this soup is an ideal starter for any meal. The sharp flavours of ginger and garlic merge beautifully with the fresh flavour of herbs like coriander and mint. Even the "one by two" option is enough, as this soup is so filling!

Preparation Time: 15 minutes. **Cooking Time:** 15 minutes. **Serves** 4.

1½ tbsp oil
1 tbsp finely chopped garlic *(lehsun)*
1 tbsp chopped ginger *(adrak)*
A pinch MSG (Mono sodium glutamate), optional
2 tbsp finely chopped tomatoes
2 tbsp finely chopped cauliflower (optional)
2 tbsp finely chopped carrots
2 tbsp finely chopped cabbage
1 tbsp finely chopped fresh mint leaves *(phudina)*
1 tbsp chopped coriander *(dhania)*
1 tbsp soya sauce
2 tsp chilli sauce
2 tsp tomato sauce
Salt and freshly ground pepper to taste
2 tbsp cornflour dissolved in ½ cup water

For serving
1 cup fried noodles, page 77
Chilli sauce
Soya sauce
Chillies in vinegar, page 77

1. Heat the oil in a wok or *kadhai* till it smokes, add the garlic and ginger and sauté on a high flame for a few seconds.
2. Add the MSG, tomatoes, cauliflower, carrots and cabbage and sauté on a high flame for another minute.
3. Add 1½ cups of water, mint leaves, coriander, soya sauce, chilli sauce, tomato sauce, salt and pepper, mix well and bring to boil.
4. Add the cornflour paste, mix well and simmer till the soup thickens.
5. Pour equal portions of soup in 4 bowls and serve immediately with fried noodles, chilli sauce, soya sauce and chillies in vinegar.

HOT AND SOUR SOUP

You can feel your taste buds shift gears from the spicy chilli sauce to the sour vinegar, creating a magical experience! A mélange of neatly chopped veggies cooked in stock and other spices makes this a wholesome treat too. Served best with crisp noodles and typical Chinese accompaniments like vinegar, chilli sauce and soya sauce.

Preparation Time: 20 minutes. **Cooking Time:** 5 to 7 minutes. **Serves** 4.

2 tbsp oil
1 tbsp finely chopped garlic *(lehsun)*
A pinch MSG (Mono sodium glutamate), optional
½ cup shredded cabbage
½ cup grated carrots
½ cup finely chopped cauliflower
¼ cup chopped spring onions
2 tbsp vinegar
1 tbsp soya sauce
1 tbsp chilli sauce
Salt and freshly ground pepper to taste
3 tbsp cornflour dissolved in ½ cup water

For serving
Chilli sauce
Soya sauce
Chillies in vinegar, page 77

1. Heat the oil in a wok or a *kadhai* till it smokes, add the garlic and MSG and sauté on a high flame for a few seconds.
2. Add the cabbage, carrots, cauliflower, spring onions and sauté on a high flame for another 2 minutes.
3. Add 4 cups of water, vinegar, soya sauce, chilli sauce, salt and pepper, mix well and simmer for 2 minutes.
4. Add the cornflour paste, mix well and simmer till the soup thickens, while stirring ocassionally.
5. Pour equal portions of soup in 4 bowls and serve immediately with chilli sauce, soya sauce and chillies in vinegar.

CHINESE BHEL

The chaat that will go down in history as the only one to be featured in a Chinese stall! And it is no rocket science! All it requires is a quick mix of minimal ingredients. Munch on these crispies when waiting for the main course.

Preparation Time: 10 minutes. **Cooking Time:** Nil. **Makes** 4 plates.

For the Schezuan sauce (makes approx. 2 cups)
½ cup oil
¼ tsp MSG (Mono sodium glutamate), optional
¼ cup finely chopped celery *(ajmoda)*
¼ cup finely chopped garlic *(lehsun)*
¼ cup finely chopped ginger *(adrak)*
½ cup tomato purée
1½ cups red chilli paste, page 63
Salt to taste
2 tbsp vinegar
2 tsp sugar

Other ingredients
4 cups fried noodles, refer handy tip, page 77
½ cup chopped spring onions (including the greens)
½ cup shredded cabbage
⅓ cup grated carrots
¼ cup thinly sliced capsicum (optional)
⅓ cup tomato sauce
⅓ cup Schezuan sauce, recipe above
Salt to taste

For the Schezuan sauce

1. Heat the oil in a *kadhai* till it smokes, add the MSG, celery, garlic and ginger, mix well and sauté on a medium flame for 30 seconds or till the flavour releases.
2. Add the tomato purée, mix well and cook on a medium flame for 4 to 5 minutes, while stirring continuously.
3. Add the red chilli paste, salt and 2 tbsp of water, mix well and simmer for a minute, while stirring continuously.
4. Add the salt, vinegar and sugar, mix well and cook on a medium flame for another minute, while stirring continuously. Use as required.

How to proceed

1. Combine all the ingredients in a bowl and toss well till the noodles are evenly coated with the sauces.
2. Place equal portions of the *bhel* on 4 plates and serve immediately.

HAKKA NOODLES

The name comes from the Hakka people the Chinese tribe that first moved to Calcutta in the late 1700s. These noodles are processed and thus don't take much time to cook. The boiled noodles and veggies are made much in advance and kept ready for the hungry diners. You just need to wait a few minutes for the noodles to be tossed!

Preparation Time: 10 minutes.   **Cooking Time:** 3 to 4 minutes.   **Makes** 4 plates.

3 tbsp oil
1 tbsp finely chopped garlic *(lehsun)*
A pinch MSG (Mono sodium glutamate), optional
½ cup chopped spring onion whites
2 medium sized capsicum, cut into long thin strips
1¼ cups shredded cabbage
¼ cup carrot juliennes
4 cups boiled noodles, refer handy tip
1 tbsp soya sauce
2 tsp vinegar (optional)
Salt and freshly ground pepper to taste
½ cup chopped spring onion greens

For serving
Chilli sauce
Soya sauce
Chillies in vinegar, page 77

1. Heat the oil in a wok or *kadhai* till it smokes, add the garlic and MSG and sauté on a high flame for a few seconds.

2. Add the spring onion whites, capsicum, cabbage and carrot and sauté on a high flame for 2 minutes.
3. Add the noodles, soya sauce, vinegar, salt, pepper and spring onion greens, toss well and sauté on a high flame for another minute.
4. Place equal portions of noodles on 4 plates and serve immediately with chilli sauce, soya sauce and chillies in vinegar.

Handy tip:

To make 4 cups of boiled noodles: Boil enough water in a deep pan, add salt, 1 tbsp of oil and 2 packets of noodles and cook till the noodles is 85% cooked. Drain using a strainer or colander and refresh using cold water. Let all the water drain out and ensure that the noodles do not contain any moisture. Spread evenly on a *thali* and keep aside to cool completely. Use as required. The quantity of cooked noodles will vary with the brand used. We have used the regular local brand, which vendors commonly use

VEG FRIED RICE

This is one dish that needs no introduction, and indeed it finds a place in every menu from the street-side to five-star eateries! Cooked rice combined with neatly cut juliennes of veggies and tossed in soya sauce. Since it's a little on the blander side, you can aptly serve with chilli sauce. Goes well with Veg Manchurian, page 75.

Preparation Time: 15 minutes. **Cooking Time:** 30 minutes. **Makes** 4 plates.

1 tbsp oil
A pinch MSG (Mono sodium glutamate), optional
1 tbsp finely chopped celery (ajmoda)
1 cup chopped spring onion whites
½ cup chopped capsicum
½ cup chopped French beans
½ cup chopped carrot
½ cup shredded cabbage
3 cups cooked rice, refer handy tip
2 tsp soya sauce
A pinch of freshly ground white pepper
1 cup chopped spring onion greens
Salt to taste

For serving
Chilli sauce
Soya sauce
Chillies in vinegar, refer handy tip, page 77
1 recipe Veg Manchurian, page 75

1. Heat the oil in a wok or *kadhai* till it smokes, add the MSG and celery and sauté on a high flame for a few seconds.
2. Add the spring onion whites, capsicum, French beans, carrots and cabbage and sauté on a high flame for another 3 to 4 minutes.
3. Add the rice, soya sauce, pepper, spring onion greens and salt, toss well and sauté on a high flame for 2 minutes.
4. Place equal portions of rice on 4 plates and serve immediately with chilli sauce, soya sauce, chillies in vinegar and veg manchurian.

Handy tip:

To make 3 cups of cooked rice: Boil enough water in a deep pan, add salt, 1 tbsp of oil and 1 cup of soaked and drained short grain rice and cook till the rice is 85% cooked. Drain using a strainer or colander and refresh using cold water. Let all the water drain out and ensure that the rice do not contain any moisture. Spread evenly on a *thali* and keep aside to cool completely. Use as required.

VEG MANCHURIAN

You cannot miss the inimitable smell of cooking garlic, onions and chillies, which will grab your attention even from 500 metres away! This ever-popular Chinese dish is really easy to make. When you eat these deep-fried vegetable balls in a soya sauce based gravy, do not let mundane things like the weighing scale bother you! Just enjoy it!

Preparation Time: 15 minutes. **Cooking Time:** 20 minutes.   **Makes** 4 plates.

For the vegetable balls
2 cups finely chopped cabbage
¼ cup grated carrots
⅓ cup finely chopped spring onions
3 tbsp cornflour
1 tbsp plain flour *(maida)*
2 tsp finely chopped garlic *(lehsun)*
1 tsp finely chopped green chillies
¼ tsp MSG (Mono sodium glutamate), optional
Salt and freshly ground pepper to taste
Oil for deep-frying

For the Manchurian sauce
2 tbsp oil
¼ tsp MSG (Mono sodium glutamate), optional
2 tsp finely chopped garlic *(lehsun)*
2 tsp finely chopped ginger *(adrak)*
1 tbsp chopped spring onions
1 tbsp chopped capsicum
2 tsp dark soya sauce

2 tbsp cornflour dissolved in 1 cup water
A pinch of freshly ground white pepper
2 pinches sugar
Salt to taste
¼ cup finely chopped spring onion greens

For serving
4 tsp spring onion greens
1 recipe Veg Fried Rice, page 74

For the vegetable balls
1. Combine all the ingredients, except the oil, in a bowl and mix well.
2. Divide the mixture into 16 equal portions and shape each portion into a round ball.
3. Heat the oil in a *kadhai* and deep-fry the balls in batches on a medium flame till they are golden brown in colour from all sides. Drain on absorbent paper and keep aside.

For the Manchurian sauce
1. Heat the oil in a wok or *kadhai* till it smokes, add the MSG, garlic, ginger, onions and capsicum and sauté on a high flame for a few seconds.
2. Add 1 cup of water, soya sauce, cornflour paste, pepper, sugar, salt and spring onion greens, mix well and simmer for another 2 minutes or till the sauce thickens. Keep aside.

How to serve
1. Just before serving, add the vegetable balls to the sauce and bring to boil.
2. Place equal portions of manchurian in 4 bowls, garnish with spring onion greens and serve hot with vegetable fried rice.

TRIPLE SCHEZUAN RICE

Combines hakka noodles, fried rice, crisp noodles and a spicy vegetable gravy in a single-layered dish! One definitely doesn't need to have anything else along with this… you will be full up to the brim. Thus, be on the safer side and buy a half-plate instead.

Preparation Time: 15 minutes. **Cooking Time:** 10 minutes. **Makes** 4 plates.

For the rice
3 tbsp oil
A pinch of MSG (Mono Sodium Glutamate), optional
1 tsp finely chopped celery *(ajmoda)*
1 tbsp finely chopped garlic *(lehsun)*
1/3 cup chopped spring onions with the greens
1/3 cup shredded cabbage
1/4 cup thinly sliced carrots
1/3 cup Schezuan sauce, page 72
3 cups cooked rice, page 74
1 cup boiled noodles, page 73, roughly chopped
2 to 3 drops orange-red food colour mixed with 1 tbsp of water
Salt to taste

For the gravy
1 tbsp oil
1/4 tsp MSG (Mono Sodium Glutamate), optional
2 tsp finely chopped garlic *(lehsun)*
1 tsp finely chopped ginger *(adrak)*
2 tbsp Schezuan sauce, page 72
1 tbsp finely chopped spring onions with the greens
1/4 cup shredded cabbage
1 tsp soya sauce
1 tsp tomato sauce
1 to 2 drops orange-red food colour mixed with 1 tbsp water
A pinch freshly ground white pepper
A pinch sugar
Salt to taste
1½ tbsp cornflour dissolved in 1 cup of water

For serving
2 cups fried noodles, page 77
Chilli sauce
Soya sauce
Chillies in vinegar, page 77

For the rice
1. Heat the oil in a wok or *kadhai* till it smokes, add the MSG and celery and sauté on a high flame for a few seconds.
2. Add the garlic and spring onions, cabbage and carrots and sauté on a high flame for 2 more minutes.
3. Add the Schezuan sauce, rice, noodles, orange-red food colour and salt, toss well and sauté on a high flame for another minute. Keep aside.

For the gravy
1. Heat the oil in a wok or *kadhai* till it smokes, add the MSG, garlic, ginger and sauté on a high flame for a few seconds.
2. Add the Schezuan sauce, spring onions and cabbage and sauté on a high flame for another minute.
3. Add 1½ cups of water, soya sauce, tomato sauce, orange-red food colour, pepper, sugar, salt and cornflour paste, mix well and simmer for another 2 minutes or till it thickens. Keep aside.

How to serve
1. Warm the rice and place equal portions on 4 plates or deep-dishes and make small depressions in the centre.
2. Pour equal quantities of hot gravy in the centre of each plate, spread ½ cup of fried noodles over the gravy in each plate. Serve immediately with chilli sauce, soya sauce and chillies in vinegar.

Handy tips:

To make 1 cup fried noodles: Heat the oil in a *kadhai* and deep-fry 1 cup of boiled noodles, page 73, in batches in hot oil till they turn golden brown in colour and crisp. Drain on absorbent paper and use as required.

To make chillies in vinegar (approx. 1 cup): Combine 1 cup of vinegar with 1 tbsp of finely chopped green chillies and cook on a slow flame for a minute. Keep aside to cool and use as required. Chillies in vinegar are served with the Chinese food and it perks up the flavour by enhancing sour and spicy taste. You can store it in a bottle and keep refrigerated for months.

Mumbai's street food caters to every meal, right from breakfast! And when you get tasty and hygienic options at just about Rs 6, what is there to complain about.

Come breakfast time, and you cannot miss the large crowds at the tiny stalls serving pohe, sheera and upma right from 7:45 up to 10 in the morning! For breakfast on the go, they also provide readymade parcels, which cater to the steady office-going crowd.

There are dozens of other quick food alternatives that you can have any time of the day. Frankies, for instance, are the essence of Mumbai street food!

They are the Indian version of wraps, if you choose to call them so. During lunch time in Mumbai, college kids will rush in hordes to their local food stall and indulge in one or several types of Frankies. What's so great about them is that they are so versatile and can be filled with anything you like. They are delicious, teenager-friendly and perfect for a snack. A unique alternative that has entered the scene recently is the Chila - Crepes made with besan or moong dal, innovatively served, sandwiched between bread and with toppings of your choice.

The Mumbai foodie will kill us if we forget to mention the Khichia papads in this context. Khichia papad is a light refreshment available in two varieties - plain and spicy (spiced with chilli flakes). Street food can be healthy too - indulge in the many various varieties of chana served with toppings like mixed veggies and chutneys. This is as healthy as roadside food can get!

Speaking of light snacks and refreshments, how can we ever forget the cart vendors stationed outside schools, selling candy floss, ber (ziziphus), karinji (star fruit), imli, tender fennel, etc. Other mobile carts include chana jor garam, peanuts, sliced cucumber served with chaat masala, etc. I'm too hungry now to go on with this list!

As for dessert options, don't fret! There is enough to satisfy the sweet tooth, ranging from malai golas to kulfis and faloodas which are very nicely and intricately presented despite the small range of ingredients available to the vendors!

How easy on the pocket: Rs. 6 to Rs. 35

A few areas you just can't afford to miss:

Indraprasth Shopping Centre, Borivali - West •
National College, Bandra • Parle (Khichia) •
Bhuleshwar • Ghatkopar • Mulund • Juhu Beach •
Kandivali Chowpatty, S. V. Road.

A Few more

VEG FRANKIE

A popular and cheap version of the hi-fi wraps and rolls! The maida roti is pre-cooked and kept ready. This is then stuffed with fillings ranging from a basic potatoes and onions mixture, to more innovative versions. The tangy taste of chillies in vinegar and chaat masala is very enjoyable! One of the most interesting and practical snacks to devour on the go!

Preparation Time: 30 minutes. **Cooking Time:** 20 minutes. **Makes** 4 frankies.

For the *rotis*
½ cup plain flour (maida)
¼ cup whole wheat flour (gehun ka atta)
1 tsp oil
Salt to taste
¼ tsp oil for kneading
Butter for cooking

For the stuffing
1½ tbsp oil/ butter
1 tsp ginger-garlic (adrak-lehsun) paste
1¾ cups boiled, peeled and mashed potatoes
¾ tsp chilli powder
1 tsp garam masala
½ tsp chaat masala (optional)
1 tbsp finely chopped coriander (dhania)
Salt to taste

To be mixed into *masala* water (makes approx ⅓ cup)
1½ tsp dried mango powder (amchur)
½ tsp chilli powder
¼ tsp garam masala
Salt to taste
⅓ cup of water

Other ingredients
4 tsp butter for cooking
1 cup finely chopped onions
4 tsp frankie masala (readily available in the market)/ chaat masala

For serving
Tomato sauce

For the *rotis*
1. Combine all the ingredients in a bowl and knead into a soft and pliable dough using enough water.
2. Cover the dough with a wet muslin cloth and keep aside for 10 minutes.
3. Knead again using ¼ tsp of oil till it is smooth and elastic.
4. Divide the dough into 4 equal portions and roll out each into approx. 200 mm. (8") diameter thin circle.
5. Heat a tava (griddle) and cook each roti lightly on a medium flame and keep aside.

For the stuffing
1. Heat the oil/butter in a kadhai, add the ginger-garlic paste and sauté on a medium flame for a few seconds.
2. Add the potatoes, chilli powder, garam masala, chaat masala, coriander and salt, mix well and sauté on a medium flame for another minute. Keep aside.

How to proceed
1. Heat ½ tsp butter on a tava (griddle), place ¼ th of the stuffing and cook on a medium flame till both sides turn light brown in colour. Keep aside.
2. Place a roti on the tava (griddle) and cook again on a medium flame using ½ tsp butter till both sides turn light brown in colour.
3. Place the stuffing on one end of the roti, spread it lightly and remove from the tava (griddle).
4. Place it on a clean, dry surface and top with ¼ cup of onions, sprinkle 1½ tsp of masala water and ½ tsp of chaat masala evenly over it and roll it up tightly.
5. Fold the edges at one end and wrap in an aluminium foil/tissue paper and serve immediately with tomato sauce.
6. Repeat with the remaining ingredients to make 3 more frankies.

VARIATIONS:

CHEESE FRANKIE

Sprinkle ⅓ cup of grated cooking cheese over the stuffing (at step no. 4, page 80) and proceed as per the recipe.

SCHEZUAN FRANKIE

Simply smear 1½ tbsp of schezuan sauce, page 72, evenly on the *roti* (after step no. 2, page 80) and proceed as per the recipe.

PANEER FRANKIE

For the stuffing, replace ¾ cup of potatoes with ¾ cup of chopped *paneer* (cottage cheese) and proceed as per the recipe, page 80.

JAIN FRANKIE

Replace potatoes with equal quantities of raw banana for the stuffing and replace onions with equal quantities of cabbage in the recipe, page 80. You can add grated cheese over the stuffing to make it more flavourful.

CHILA

Nestled amongst the busy lanes of Bhuleshwar, this Gujju snack is more famous in the south of Mumbai. It is slowly spreading its wings to the other regions too. It is made with besan batter but can also be made with moong dal batter. The simplest fare is made with butter and coriander. For elaborate versions, experiment with paneer, cheese, tomato, etc.

Preparation Time: 10 minutes. **Cooking Time:** 15 minutes. **Makes** 4 plates.
Soaking Time: 1 hour.

To be mixed together into a smooth batter
¾ cup *besan* (Bengal gram flour)
3 tbsp yellow *moong dal* (split yellow gram), soaked and ground into a paste
¼ tsp carom seeds *(ajwain)*
¼ tsp turmeric powder *(haldi)*
¼ tsp chilli powder
¼ tsp finely chopped green chillies (optional)
A pinch asafoetida *(hing)*
2 tsp oil
Salt to taste
¾ cup water

Other ingredients
¼ tsp oil for greasing
2 tsp finely chopped coriander *(dhania)*
2 tbsp butter for cooking

For serving
Meetha chutney, page 10
Teekha chutney, page 10
Geela lehsun ka chutney, page 18
½ cup finely chopped onions
4 bread slices

1. Heat a non-stick *tava* (griddle) on a medium flame and grease it lightly with oil.
2. Pour ¼th portion of the mixture on it and spread it evenly using a ladle to make a thin circle of approx. 225 mm. (9") in diameter.
3. Sprinkle ½ tsp of coriander and smear ½ tbsp of butter evenly over it using a spatula.
4. Cook on a medium flame till the *chila* turns golden brown in colour on one side.

5. Turn over, cook on a medium flame for another minute and fold over using a spatula to make a semi-circle.
6. Place the *chila* on a plate and serve immediately with *meetha chutney, teekha chutney, geela lehsun ka chutney,* ¼th of the onions and a bread slice.
7. Repeat with the remaining ingredients to make 3 more plates.

FARALI PATTICE

Who says a person cannot feast when fasting! Faral means "fast" and these pattice are designed specifically for those who are fasting. The coating of arrowroot flour adds a unique dimension to this otherwise common dish. Serve with sweetened curds, to complete the masti experience!

Preparation Time: 15 minutes.   **Cooking Time:** 10 to 12 minutes.   **Makes** 4 plates (8 *pattice*).

To be mixed together into a potato mixture
1¾ cups boiled, peeled and mashed potatoes
3 tbsp arrowroot flour
Salt to taste

To be mixed together into a stuffing
⅓ cup freshly grated coconut
3 tbsp peanuts, roasted and powdered
3 tbsp finely chopped coriander *(dhania)*
1½ tsp chopped raisins *(kismis)*
1½ tsp chopped cashewnuts *(kaju)*
1 tbsp ginger-green chilli paste
1½ tbsp sugar
1 tbsp of lemon juice
Salt to taste

To be mixed together into sweetened curds
1 cup chilled fresh curds *(dahi)*, beaten
3 tbsp powdered sugar
A pinch salt (optional)

Other ingredients
Arrowroot flour for coating
Oil for deep-frying

For serving
Teekha chutney, page 10
Sweetened curds, recipe above

1. Divide the potato mixture and the stuffing each into 8 equal portions and keep aside.
2. Flatten a portion of the potato mixture into a 75 mm. (3") diameter circle and place a portion of the stuffing in the centre.
3. Bring together the edges in the centre to seal the stuffing and shape it into a round ball. Keep aside.
4. Repeat with the remaining potato mixture and stuffing to make 7 more *pattice*.
5. Roll the *pattice* in the arrowroot flour till they are evenly coated from all the sides.
6. Heat the oil in a *kadhai* and deep-fry the *pattice* on a medium flame till they turn light brown in colour from all the sides. Drain on absorbent paper.

How to serve
1. Place 2 *farali pattice* on a plate and serve immediately with *teekha chutney* and sweetened curds.
2. Repeat with the remaining ingredients to make 3 more plates.

ALOO CHAAT

It's a delight to watch the baby potato turn into something so exciting! Tiny potatoes, marinated in Indian spices and sautéed in oil, are served topped with curds and delicious chaat toppings. Not an integral part of all chaat counters, but has a fan-following of its own.

Preparation Time: 20 minutes.   **Cooking Time:** 2 to 3 minutes.   **Makes** 4 plates.

For the *masala aloo*
2 tbsp coriander-cumin seeds *(dhania-jeera)* powder
2 tsp chilli powder
2 tsp *besan* (Bengal gram flour)
2 tsp dry mango powder *(amchur)*
¼ tsp turmeric powder *(haldi)*
2 tbsp oil
Salt to taste
12 baby potatoes, boiled and peeled

add - that pen
chickpeas
temrind paste

For serving
1 cup fresh curds *(dahi)*, beaten
6 tbsp *meetha chutney*, page 10
8 tsp *teekha phudina chutney*, page 22
4 tsp *geela lehsun ka chutney*, page 18
½ cup boiled *moong* (whole green gram) sprouts
1 tsp dry *masala* powder, page 22
6 tbsp Nylon *sev*, page 19 / mixed *farsan*, refer handy tip
4 tsp *masala dal*, page 23
4 tsp finely chopped coriander *(dhania)*

For the *masala aloo*
1. Combine the coriander-cumin seeds powder, chilli powder, *besan*, salt, dry mango powder, turmeric powder, 1 tbsp of oil and salt in a bowl and mix well.

2. Add the potatoes and mix well till they are evenly coated. Keep aside to marinate for 5 to 7 minutes.
3. Heat the remaining 1 tbsp of oil in a *kadhai,* add the marinated potatoes and cook on a medium flame for 2 to 3 minutes, while stirring gently. Keep aside.

How to serve
1. Place 3 *masala aloo* on a plate and mash them lightly.
2. Top with ¼ cup of curds, 1½ tbsp of *meetha chutney*, 2 tsp of *teekha phudina chutney* and 1 tsp of *geela lehsun ka chutney*.
3. Sprinkle 1½ tbsp of *moong* and sprinkle ¼ tsp of dry *masala* powder, 1½ tbsp of *sev* / mixed *farsan*, 1 tsp of *masala dal* and 1 tsp of coriander evenly over it and serve immediately.
4. Repeat with the remaining ingredients to make 3 more plates.

Handy tip:
Mixed *farsan* is a combination of *sev, papdi, teekha gathiya* and *chivda*. It is readily available in the market.

SHEERA

A sweet, but had as part of breakfast by seasoned Mumbaikars. Though high in calories, it is quite low when it comes to the price, at just Rs. 7 per plate! You cannot miss the vendors selling sheera in huge stainless steel vessels and returning within an hour after selling every morsel.

Preparation Time: 5 minutes. **Cooking Time:** 20 minutes. **Makes** 4 plates.
Soaking Time: 10 to 15 minutes.

⅓ cup ghee
1 cups semolina *(rawa/sooji)*
½ cup warm milk
1 cup sugar
1 tbsp chopped raisins *(kismis)*
1 tbsp chopped cashewnuts *(kaju)*
½ tsp cardamom *(elaichi)* powder

1. Heat the ghee in a *kadhai,* add the semolina and sauté on a slow flame for 5 to 7 minutes. Keep aside.
2. Add the milk and ½ cup of warm water, mix well and simmer for 3 to 4 minutes or till all the liquid evaporates, while stirring continuously.
3. Add the sugar, raisins, cashewnuts and cardamom, mix well and cook on a slow flame and the *sheera* leaves the sides of the *kadhai,* stirring once in between.
4. Place equal quantites of *sheera* on 4 plates and serve immediately.

DRY FRUIT GOLA

Golas, made from crushed ice laced with sherbets of different flavours, are a relief from the scorching heat. Crushing machines keep churning out the ice, to be merged with various flavours like kala khatta, rose, mango... name it and they have it! Don't forget to have the Milkmaid gola made with condensed milk or the very interesting Cadbury gola.

Preparation Time: 10 minutes.   **Cooking Time:** 15 to 20 minutes.   **Makes** 4 dryfruit *gola*.

For the *rabadi* (makes approx. 2 cups)
3 cups milk
½ cup sugar
¾ cup grated *mava (khoya)*

Other ingredients
8 cups ice cubes
6 tbsp pineapple syrup (readily available in the market)
4 tbsp rose syrup (readily available in the market)
4 tbsp orange syrup (readily available in the market)
4 tbsp *kala khatta* syrup (readily available in the market)
4 tbsp *kacchi kairi* syrup (readily available in the market)
6 tbsp chopped mixed nuts (cashewnuts, raisins, pistachios etc.)
6 tbsp grated *mava (khoya)*

For the *rabadi*
1. Boil the milk in a deep pan, add the sugar and simmer till it reduces to half its quantity, while stirring continuously.
2. Add the *mava*, mix well and simmer for another 2 minutes, while stirring continuously. Keep aside to cool and keep refrigerated till required.

How to proceed
1. Place 2 cups of ice cubes in an ice-crushing machine (refer handy tip) and crush till fine.
2. Place the crushed ice in a bowl, press it and unmould on a serving plate.
3. Pour 1½ tbsp of pineapple syrup evenly over it.
4. Pour ½ cup of *rabadi* and sprinkle 1½ tbsp of *mava* evenly over it.
5. Pour 1 tbsp each of rose syrup, orange syrup, *kala khatta* syrup and *kacchi kairi* syrup evenly over it.
6. Sprinkle 1½ tbsp of nuts evenly over it and serve immediately.
7. Repeat with the remaining ingredients to make 3 more dryfruit *gola*.

Handy tip:
In the absence of an ice-crushing machine, lay out a clean towel and cover half of it with ice-cubes/cracked ice pieces. Fold the other half of the cloth over it, and then crush the ice coarsely using a rolling pin. Use immediately.

FALOODA

Distinctly flavoured with rose syrup, this is one dessert which is not to be missed. You will find ready-dried falooda sev in the market, which just needs to be soaked before use. A perfect finish to a light meal. For a royal fanfare try the Royal Falooda- falooda loaded with dried fruits and jelly.

Preparation Time: 10 minutes. **Cooking Time:** Nil. **Makes** 4 *faloodas*.

6 tbsp rose syrup
4 tsp soaked garden cress seeds (*subza*)
4 tbsp soaked *falooda sev,* refer handy tip no.1
4 tbsp chopped strawberry flavoured jelly, refer handy tip no.2
4 cups chilled milk
4 scoops of vanilla ice-cream (readily available in the market)

For the garnish
4 tsp chopped strawberry flavoured jelly

1. Place 1½ tbsp of rose syrup in a glass, top with 1 tsp of garden cress seeds, 1 tbsp of *falooda sev* and 1 tbsp of jelly.
2. Pour 1 cup of milk over it gently so that the milk does not mix with the syrup, refer handy tip no. 3.
3. Top with a scoop of ice-cream, garnish with 1 tsp of jelly and serve immediately.
4. Repeat with the remaining ingredients to make 3 more *falooda.*

VARIATION:
KULFI FALOODA

1. Cut a *kulfi* (readily available in the market) into 4 equal pieces and place them on a plate.
2. Top with 1 tsp of garden cress seeds, ½ tbsp of *falooda sev* and 1 tbsp of rose syrup and serve immediately.

Handy tips:

1. *Falooda sev* packet *is* readily available in the market. The *sev* needs to be soaked in water and drained. Use as required.
2. To make strawberry flavoured jelly, follow the instructions on the packet. Use the quantities as required in this recipe and remaining as required.
3. Place an inverted tbsp/dessert spoon at a 45° angle over the glass and pour the milk over the spoon. The milk will slide gently to form a layer over the syrup and won't get mixed with it.

As divinely as a meal might be, it turns sour when you do not have fluids to accompany it! You will be amazed at the brilliant variety of accompaniments that Mumbai's streets offer. Whether it is a hot cup of cutting chai or chilled chaas, nimboo pani, ganne ka ras and sodas, you will find it all on the streets of our city, and at a really moderate price of Rs. 4 to Rs. 10. If you don't have the place in your tummy for an entire glass, ask for half a glass or have a "One by Two" with your friend!

When it comes to beverages, nariyal pani has always been a hot favourite in Mumbai. Once you are done with the nariyal pani, you can ask the vendor to cut open the coconut and give you the malai or tender coconut, which he scoops out using a piece of the coconut shell itself. This comes at a modest price of Rs. 12 to Rs. 15.

With good health coming into the spotlight, fruit and vegetable juices are also available everywhere and are a really great way to beat the heat. Fruits serve as another healthy alternative that quenches not just thirst but also a mild hunger pang. You will find vendors neatly cutting fruits and placing an assortment on each plate. With a sprinkling of chaat masala, the fruit plate becomes a healthy and tangy refreshment. And all this at just Rs. 5 to Rs. 12 (depending on the area).

For those who are not that health-conscious and would rather go for sweet refreshments, Mewad ice cream carts are there in almost every part of the city. If you are not in the mood for ice cream, indulge in the goodness of freshly-made jalebis, kulfi, etc or indulge in sweetened beverages like lassi, ice-cream, masala milk, kesar doodh, rose milk, milkshakes with ice-cream, etc.

How easy on the pocket: Rs. 4 to Rs. 30 (depending on the preparation)

A few areas you just can't afford to miss:

Amar Juice Centre, Parle • Churchgate Station • Juhu Beach • Chowpatty • Borivali • Cutting Chai, National College • Bandra • Sardar Gola, Ghatkopar.

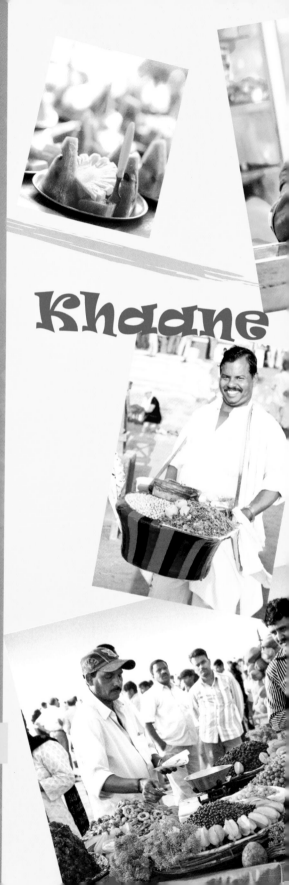

Khaane

Saath

Ke

Tarla Dalal's
Indian Collection

Non-fried Snacks

South Indian Recipes

Mughlai Khana

The Complete
Gujarati Cook Book

Soya Rotis & Subzis

Rajasthani Cookbook

Punjabi Khana

Desi Khana

Chaat

Swadisht Subzian

Mithai

Tava Cooking

Rotis & Subzis

Achaar Aur Parathe

Kebabs & Tikkis

Microwave Desi Khana

Chawal

Curries & Kadhis

Paneer

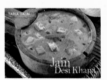

Jain Desi Khana

Roz Ka Khana

Dals

Healthy Subzis

Punjabi Subzis

Parathas